PLUGGED IN
TO
ENGLISH

John O. Cole

Cottonwood Press, Inc.
Fort Collins, Colorado

Requests for permission should be addressed to:

email: cottonwood@cottonwoodpress.com
phone: 1-800-864-4297
fax: 970-204-0761

Cottonwood Press, Inc.
107 Cameron Drive
Fort Collins, Colorado 80525

ISBN 1-877673-60-9

Printed in the United States of America

COTTONWOOD PRESS INC.

www.cottonwoodpress.com

Acknowledgments

This work would never have come to completion without the support of my wife Robyn, whose assurances buoyed me and whose criticism and praise encouraged me.

Others I am indebted to include dedicated West Liberty State College English colleagues Sally Coyne, Peggy Griswold, Linda McGinley, Mary Rogerson, and Kathy Paleudis, who listened patiently to my effusive talk about this book for the past year and willingly tried exercises; a trio of talented Brooke High School teachers – Candice Owens, Janet Piccirillo, and Carolyn Shaffer; my West Virginia English Language Arts Council associates, who praised my first attempts to write computer lab exercises; and hundreds of my freshman composition and English methods students, who were my experimental group for years. I am deeply indebted to them, not only for their criticism and creative suggestions, but also for their inspiration. The enthusiasm they exhibited when they were engaged in lab activities rewarded me and challenged me to create more.

Finally, this book is also a product of four astute advisors and diligent proofreaders – my wife Robyn, my daughter Devon, and friends Ruth Westlake of Bethany College and Kathy Paleudis of West Liberty. Last but not least, I thank Rosey Miller, Media Director at West Liberty, who jovially tolerated all my demands on her time as she assisted me in printing the many drafts.

Table of Contents

The computer is so much more than a fancy typewriter

A 1998 article in *T.H.E. Journal,* a publication of Technological Horizons in Education, stated that many educators regard costly computer networks as a "dubious 'bells and whistles' distraction from basic education."

I am not one of those individuals. I wholeheartedly embrace the use of computers in the language arts classroom.

The computer lab, despite its popular face-to-the-wall layout, creates an environment that is invigorating and stimulating, one that nurtures the processes of oral and written language. Old activities become new and different when used in a computer lab. The dynamic nature of word processing software allows the creation of new activities that invite and challenge students who have grown weary of fill-in-the-blank workbook exercises.

I have sought new ways to use the computer lab in teaching writing and literature – ways that go far beyond having students plan an essay and then type it as though the computer were nothing more than a fancy typewriter. Observing students tackle meaningful computer-based exercises each week, I have noted the following:

- Following lab activities, students who are usually quiet during class discussions are often eager to participate and frequently make significant contributions.

- Students display their creative instincts more frequently than in the traditional classroom setting.

- Students are self-directed as long as I have clearly defined the task. (I often learn how to improve the directions or the scope of the assignment from students whose computer literacy is greater than mine.)

- Students' computer skills increase significantly.

The use of computers in language arts has reinvigorated me as a teacher, so much so that I look forward to reading and sharing students' responses with colleagues and my wife. Yes, there are days when the system goes down, when computers lock up, when disruptions in electrical service wipe out the work, but those inconveniences are nothing compared to the renewed enthusiasm students bring to the language arts classroom.

John Cole

COMPUTER TIPS

FOR

LANGUAGE ARTS
TEACHERS

What if you're *not* a computer guru?

Unfortunately, many people assume that language arts teachers have a thorough understanding of computers, particularly basic maintenance procedures and word processing programs. How such a misconception developed is easy to imagine. Word processing programs are the most visible and widely used in public education. Because language arts teachers are specifically trained in language and literature skills, both administrators and the general public often assume that they are also computer "gurus."

What few realize, however, is that word processing became a significant component of language arts teacher education programs only in the last decade. As most teachers were trained earlier – sometimes decades earlier – few of them have actually become computer experts. The two main reasons are time and money. Too few schools can afford to offer computer literacy training, and even fewer language arts teachers can afford to purchase the latest computer technology to keep them on the cutting edge.

If you are a teacher who is *not* a computer guru, the tips that follow will hardly catapult you to the head of the class. However, they will help you lead computer lab exercises successfully. Yes, there will still be those student computer savants who will remind you of how little you know and understand about computers. However, these students can often become your best free consultants!

Tips for the computer lab

Learn lab policy. Before you take your class into the computer lab, become familiar with the lab policies at your school. See the box on page 12 for items on a typical list.

If the computer lab has no set policies, adopt some of your own and post copies in the computer lab. Then provide each student with a copy and discuss the importance of each policy for constructive, productive use of the computer lab.

Get to know the lab director and assistants. It is wise to get to know your school's computer lab director, if there is one, and any lab assistants, who may be extremely knowledgeable students. These people can provide invaluable help.

Stress the importance of learning how to save properly. One of the worst problems in a computer lab is the loss or disappearance of a document. A key factor in assuring at least partial recovery of documents is teaching students how to save.

Although it may seem wise to have lab computers already set to save automatically, or to create backup copies, it is not at all practical to do so. Such features require a great deal more memory than most labs can handle. Also, problems arise when students don't understand the automatic functions.

It is a better idea to have students learn how to protect and save their work themselves. To minimize loss, to help undo mistakes, and to recover at least partial documents, students should learn the following procedures during the very first labs of the year.

- **Save**. When working on a computer, it is important to save and to save often. School computer labs often have strict procedures for where and how students save their files. To make sure students don't lose data, learn your computer lab's policy and insist that students follow it. Some computer labs will delete files saved in the wrong place.

  Generally, it is wise to have students save their work to their own floppy diskette or CD, even if other methods of saving are in place.

- **AutoRecover or AutoSave**. AutoRecover, also known as AutoSave, is a tool that saves a document automatically every few minutes. This safety feature helps prevent users from losing their work, or at least most of it, if the power goes out, the network goes down or a computer crashes. Students can set this feature themselves when they start to work, choosing how often they want a document to be automatically saved. For important documents, saving every five to ten minutes is not unreasonable.

SAMPLE COMPUTER LAB POLICY

- Computers are available on a first-come, first-served basis, unless reserved for a scheduled class or program.

- Academic work *always* takes precedence over all other uses of the computers.

- Software may be copied to or from lab computers only by the lab director.

- Food and drinks are prohibited in the lab.

- The lab director may dismiss any user from the lab for excessive noise or disruptive, unruly behavior.

- Any user who steals will be held accountable and will lose lab privileges.

- Computers may not be used for games, unless assigned by an instructor.

- Neither the school nor the lab director is responsible for any items left in the computer lab. This includes student IDs, books, and personal items.

- Neither the school nor the lab director is responsible for work left unattended on a computer, or for problems caused by computer viruses, improper use of the equipment, or loss of data due to equipment malfunctions.

(In Microsoft Word, click on Tools and select Options, then the Save tab. Set the number of minutes for AutoRecover.)

If a power failure occurs and AutoRecover or AutoSave has been set to save every 10 minutes, users will lose only the data created in the last 10 minutes. All other work will have been saved automatically. It is generally easy to recover work that has been automatically saved in a word processing program.

(To recover a document in Microsoft Word, restart the computer and Open Microsoft Word. Before it opens, a message may appear, asking if you want to view the saved version of the document that was on the screen when the power failure occurred. Click Yes. In some older versions of Microsoft Word, the document may simply appear. To verify that the version on the screen is a later version than the one you had saved, open the saved version. Once you are satisfied that the recovered version is the preferred one, click Save As, choosing the name you have been using all along for the document. If you were working on more than one file at the time of the power failure, you must repeat these steps for each file in use. Any recovered files you haven't saved will be deleted once you close Microsoft Word.)

Teach students to use "Control" shortcuts. Control (Ctrl) shortcuts allow students to make computer commands without removing their hands from the keyboard to use the mouse. They simply type the Ctrl key plus a designated letter of the alphabet. *(On Macintosh computers, the ⌘ key is used instead of Ctrl.)* Memorizing some of the commands can really speed up a person's work. Many of the combinations are quite easy to remember because the designated letter is the first letter of the word for the task desired. For example, Ctrl + b stands for BOLD. Ctrl + c stands for COPY.

In recent computer programs, Ctrl functions are usually posted beside the action in the drop-down lists in the menu bar. On some of the latest keyboards, shortcut combinations are also noted on the keys themselves.

See the chart on page 14 for a list of frequently used Ctrl functions, which are becoming universal to almost all computer programs.

Learn to troubleshoot "Control" shortcuts. Knowing shortcut commands can help you analyze mishaps that occur when students create documents. Often, in attempting to capitalize the first letter of a sentence or a proper noun, students strike the Ctrl key instead of the Shift key, thereby executing a command never intended. You can usually determine what shortcut command was mistakenly used by looking at the result.

For example, if the student suddenly finds the typeface is now bold, then Ctrl+b was probably the shortcut, an accident that occurred when the student's finger missed the Shift key and hit the Ctrl key instead. Or if a Find and Replace window opens frequently, the student is hitting Ctrl + f instead of Shift + f. (Ctrl + f means "Find.")

Another frequent problem is the accidental use of the Ctrl + n command. When students suddenly find themselves looking at a blank page, it is usually correct to assume that they have accidentally typed the Ctrl+ n command. To see if this is true, click on Window and see if a new document as well as the original shows up in the drop-down menu. If so, close the new document. The original will, of course, reappear.

COMMON "CTRL" KEY SHORTCUTS

[On Macintosh computers, use the ⌘ key instead of the Ctrl key]
Listed below are the actions possible when using "Ctrl + another key" combinations.

Ctrl + a = Highlight entire document

Ctrl + b = Bold all letters

Ctrl + c = Copy any highlighted text

Ctrl + d = Change font size, color, etc.

Ctrl + e = Center a paragraph

Ctrl + f = Find specific words, formatting or special items

Ctrl + g = Go to a page or bookmark

Ctrl + h = Replace text

Ctrl + i = Make letters italic

Ctrl + j = Justify a paragraph

Ctrl + k = Insert Hyperlink

Ctrl + l = Left align a paragraph

Ctrl + m = Indent a paragraph from left

Ctrl + n = Create a new document

Ctrl + o = Open a document

Ctrl + p = Print document

Ctrl + q = Remove paragraph formatting

Ctrl + r = Right align a paragraph

Ctrl + s = Save a document

Ctrl + t = Create a hanging indent

Ctrl + u = Underline letters

Ctrl + v = Paste text or object

Ctrl + w = Close a document

Ctrl + x = Cut the selected text or object

Ctrl + y = Redo the last action

Ctrl + z = Undo the last action

Ctrl + 0 (Zero) = Add or remove one line space preceding a paragraph

Ctrl + 1 = Single space lines

Ctrl + 2 = Double space lines

Ctrl +] = Increase font size by 1 point

Ctrl + [= Decrease font size by 1 point

Ctrl + / = Move between master and sub-documents

Ctrl + left arrow = Move cursor one word to the left

Ctrl + hyphen = Create a nonbreaking hyphen

Ctrl + right arrow = Move cursor one word to the right

Ctrl + up arrow = Move cursor one paragraph up

Ctrl + down arrow =Move cursor one paragraph down

Ctrl + spacebar = Remove character formatting

One of the easiest ways to troubleshoot a problem is to simply click on Edit. Most programs have an Undo feature. The student's last action will be listed at the top of the drop-down menu. Clicking that item will usually undo any unintentional last command.

(Note: In Microsoft Word, Ctrl + n will not show up in the Edit menu as something the student can Undo. The only way to check to see if Ctrl + n has been accidentally used is to see if a new document has been created in another window.)

Teach students to save multiple versions of a text. When students are working on lengthy documents such as research papers, it is imperative that they save multiple versions of the text. Why? They may discover that the revision they made one day is not as effective as an earlier version. Unless earlier versions are regularly saved, they are lost.

The simplest way to save multiple versions is to save work under different file names. For example, if a student is working on an essay about "friends," he might save his work on subsequent days with these file names:

- Friends Essay 3_13_2003
- Friends Essay 3_14_2003
- Friends Essay 3_15_2003
- Friends Essay 3_16_2003

Note that the month, day, and year of revision are separated by an underscore, which is a common file-naming convention. Many word processing programs will not allow symbols like the diagonal slash in file names.

Teach students to repair work by using "Undo." Emphasize to your lab students that whenever they are dissatisfied with something they have written or added to a document, either intentionally or by error, the quickest way to undo the error is usually by using the Edit feature and undoing what they have just done. In most programs, simply typing Ctrl + z will undo whatever command was just used. Many programs also have an Undo icon on the toolbar. Clicking this icon will undo the last action.

(In Microsoft Word, students can also click on Edit. Whatever appears at the top of the drop-down menu is usually the last action performed. For example, if they just typed something, Undo typing is what will appear. To correct an error, they simply click on Undo. They can click it as many times as they like to bring the document back to where they want it. Of course, they can also type Ctrl + Z, for an even faster approach.)

Teach students to use bookmarking. Bookmarking saves time in accessing frequently used Internet sites. To bookmark favorite web sites, follow the directions for the browsers being used.

(In Microsoft Internet Explorer, go to the menu and click on **Favorites**. *In Netscape Navigator, click on* **Bookmarks**.*)*

Teach students to view "Format features."

In most word processing programs, users can enable a feature that allows them to view formatting features like spaces, tab characters, and paragraph marks. Using this feature prevents a lot of errors in proofreading because it is easy to see and correct errors like extra spaces between words.

(To activate this feature in Microsoft Word, go to **Tools** *in the menu bar, select* **Options**, *then* **View**. *Under* **Formatting features** *or* **Formatting marks**, *put a check mark beside the features to be revealed, or check the* **All** *box to reveal all of them. In earlier versions of Microsoft Word, choose* **Nonprinting characters** *under* **View**.

You may also want to have students check **Hidden text**. *Sometimes when a document is scanned and copied into another document, hidden text — e.g. line breaks or other formatting commands — are also installed. Such line breaks sometimes distort the spacing and cause quirky rearrangements in a new document. If* **Hidden text** *is not selected as a feature to be revealed, it is sometimes hard to find and delete the offending commands.)*

Teach students to save time by using "Replace" to correct errors.

It's easy to find and replace errors throughout a document with the **Replace** function. Students can learn to find and replace both words and formatting commands.

In most programs, **Search** or **Find** is listed under **Edit** on the menu. After selecting what they want to find in a document, students then choose what they want to replace it with. For example, suppose that the word "editorial" has been mistakenly capitalized throughout a document. Students can search for "Editorial" and replace with "editorial." They can replace one item at a time, or they can choose **Replace All** to change all items at once.

(Earlier versions of Microsoft Word ask to **Find what** *and* **Replace with**. *Later versions ask* **Change what format?** *and* **Replace what format?**)*

Teach students how to use "Word Count."

Word Count counts the number of words in an article or other piece of writing. If you are using freewriting as a warm-up exercise to increase writing fluency, **Word Count** can quickly demonstrate to students any progress made in fluency over a period of time.

(To find **Word Count** *in Microsoft Word, click on* **Tools**, *then* **Word Count** *in the drop-down menu. The* **Word Count** *box will appear and provide statistics on number of pages, words, characters, paragraphs, and lines in the file. To count the words in only one part of a file,* **Highlight** *that area before selecting* **Word Count**.*)*

Use caution with "Spelling and Grammar" checks. The Spelling and Grammar check features in a word processing program can be useful, but you need to warn students that the features are fallible.

In Microsoft Word, for example, misspelled words are highlighted with a wavy red line. However, *any* words that are not part of the software's dictionary will be highlighted. Specialized or technical vocabulary, as well as surnames, will be highlighted as incorrect.

(In Microsoft Word, if certain words are used frequently, students may want to install them in the custom dictionary by right clicking on the word and choosing Add. *It is also possible to customize how the feature works by choosing* Tools, *then* Options, *then the* Spelling & Grammar *tab, and then selecting different items. For example, checking the box marked* Ignore words in UPPERCASE, *means that proper nouns will not be highlighted as misspelled when you do a* Spelling and Grammar *check.)*

A more common problem with Spelling check is that it doesn't recognize words that are spelled correctly, but *used* incorrectly. For example, in the sentence "Eye will bee late four the track meat," Spelling check will not find anything wrong. Students need to be reminded that they can't rely on Spelling check completely; they must also check spelling on their own.

Grammar check can prove particularly troublesome for students to use, so it may be wise to deactivate the feature. In theory, Grammar check highlights only passages with grammar, usage, punctuation, spacing, and/or syntax errors. The problem is that the program deems sophisticated sentence constructions grammatically incorrect. Worse, the solutions suggested can turn a well-wrought sentence into one that is ungrammatical.

However, if students are capable of recognizing and rejecting the misinformation in a Grammar check, the feature can be useful.

(In Microsoft Word, click on Tools, *then* Options. *Select the* Spelling & Grammar *tab. Check the box beside each feature of spelling and grammar you wish to have activated.)*

Use the Readability feature with care. The Readability feature of some word processing programs can help gauge students' development as writers by identifying style characteristics in their writing.

The reliability of the Readability feature is certainly questionable. However, used cautiously, it can provide a quick stylistic analysis of the document a student has just created. It will summarize information like the average number of sentences per paragraph, words per sentence, and sentences per document. It will also give the approximate reading level of the material created.

(To activate the Readability *feature in Microsoft Word, choose* Tools, *then* Options. *Select the* Spelling & Grammar *tab. Then check the box beside* Show readability sta-

tistics. To use the Readability *feature, highlight the material you wish to check. Choose* Tools, *then* Spelling and Grammar. *At the end of the* Spelling and Grammar *check, the* Readability Statistics *will appear. Microsoft Word gives the Flesch reading level and the Flesch-Kincaid grade level rankings for the material.)*

The Readability feature can also be used to head off unintentional plagiarism. Generally, when students use information from library or Internet sources in their documents, the reading grade level escalates. This may be an indication of plagiarism, especially in those passages where students have attempted to rephrase ideas from library or Internet sources but the words are polysyllabic and the sentences are very long — characteristics not typical of their usual style.

Teach students to use the "Thesaurus." Using the Thesaurus feature on a word processing program is usually much easier and quicker than using an actual thesaurus. It is a quick and easy way for students to find synonyms.

(In Microsoft Word, with the cursor on the word in question, click on Tools, Language, *and then* Thesaurus. *Or, more simply, just hit* Shift F7. *The Thesaurus choices should appear.)*

Teach students to use "Highlight" to mark passages that need attention later. When students are in the frenzy of drafting, they should not spend excessive amounts of time rewriting or editing. Instead, they can use the Highlight feature to call attention to words they know they don't know how to spell or passages they know they need to rephrase and rewrite later.

(In Microsoft Word, click on the Highlight *icon — a pen with a colored line under it — on the* Toolbar. *The mouse then becomes a highlighting pen. Click in front of the text you wish to highlight and drag the cursor over the word, phrases, or sentences you want to identify.* Highlight *will remain active until you click it again.*

If the Highlight *icon does not appear on the* Toolbar, *it can be added easily, as can numerous other editing and formatting features, by going to* Tools, *clicking on* Customize, *and then choosing the* Commands *tab. Highlight* Format. *Then scroll down and click on the* Highlight *icon. It will appear on the* Toolbar.

You can change the color of the highlight by clicking on the caret beside the icon on the Toolbar. *A drop-down color chart will appear. Click on the color you prefer.)*

WOES OF SPELLING AND GRAMMAR CHECKS

Spelling

- Provides several possibilities to substitute for misspellings but often selects the worst choice from the list.

- Gives no suggestion for words with several letters incorrect, so the writer has no idea how to correct the misspelling.

- Does not recognize most proper names, foreign words, or technical vocabulary.

- Does not recognize typing errors resulting in the spelling of legitimate words. Example: "form" for "from."

- Cannot distinguish between homonyms frequently misused by student writers. Example: "there, their, and they're."

- Does not catch misuse of the apostrophe in possessives. Example: "the Cole's home" instead of "the Coles' home."

Grammar

- Cannot evaluate inverted sentence order as in passive voice or subjunctive constructions. Example: It rejects the passive construction in Joyce Kilmer's line, "Poems are made by fools like me," and suggests that it be changed to, "Fools like me make poems."

- Faults legitimate long sentences because it automatically labels any lengthy construction as problematic.

- Fails to recognize faulty pronoun use as in "Me and my computer is good friends," suggesting only that the verb be changed – or sometimes suggesting that only the order be changed, as in "My computer and me is good friends."

- Often recognizes legitimate faults in sentence structure but either suggests no correction or suggests one that makes the sentence even more difficult to understand.

How should a teacher deal with Internet safety issues?

The risks. Parents sometimes ask, "Why do teachers develop activities requiring the use of the Internet when such activities can expose students to undesirable subject matter or make them vulnerable to sexual predators?" The answer is a simple one: the benefits far outweigh the risks.

What are the risks? The main ones are:

- **exposure** to inappropriate material: commercial sites with sexually explicit material; personal web pages designed to lure young people into chat rooms; racist or bigoted sites developed by hate groups; sites containing slanted or erroneous information.

- **harassment** by way of e-mails.

- **abduction and physical molestation** made possible by gaining confidence of the victim through e-mails, chat rooms, and bulletin boards.

- **legal and financial violations** resulting from using credit cards without permission or agreeing to some action that is a violation of another's rights.

How great are the risks? According to *SafeKids.Com*, the web site of the Online Safety Project created by Larry Magid, a syndicated columnist for the *Los Angeles Times* and author of numerous online safety articles, the risks for children are few but increase when they become teenagers. That's because teenagers are generally not supervised in their use of the Internet. As *SafeKids.Com* explains, "Although there have been some highly publicized cases of abuse involving the Internet and online services, reported cases are relatively infrequent." (It also acknowledges that there are a number of unreported cases, as is true of all crimes against individuals.)

Protecting young people. Given the seriousness of the risks, what can be done to protect children from them? To provide a safety net for young Internet visitors, some school libraries have installed software that filters or blocks unsavory material. While such software provides some security, students often spend little time on school computers. Most of their work is done at home or in public libraries where they may not be supervised.

SafeKids.Com and other agencies dedicated to online safety give advice on the best way to educate parents, teachers, the public, and children about the risks of using the Internet and how to avoid falling victim to them. Children need to learn "netiquette," the term for responsible behavior while using the Internet. (See page 23 for a list of guidelines.) They should also learn rules for safe use of the Internet. *SafeKids.Com* has an excellent "Kids' Rules for Online Safety" that includes items like these:

- I will not give out personal information such as my address, telephone number, parents' work address/telephone number, or the name and location of my school without my parents' permission.

- I will tell my parents right away if I come across any information that makes me feel uncomfortable when using the Internet.

- I will never agree to get together with someone I "meet" online without first checking with my parents. If my parents agree to the meeting, I will be sure that it is in a public place and bring my mother or father along.

Free copies of the entire list of "Kids' Rules for Online Safety," adapted from the brochure "Child Safety on the Information Highway," by *SafeKids.Com* founder Larry Magid, are available by calling 1-800-843-5678.

(Note: The National Center for Missing and Exploited Children provides financial support for the booklets "Child Safety on the Information Highway" and "Teen Safety on the Information Highway," accessible from the *SafeKids.Com* home page. You can also order a free copy of "Teen Safety on the Information Highway" by calling 1-800-843-5678. Another source of information is *SafeTeens.Com*, a project of The Online Safety Project [OSP].)

Proper search methods. It is important that teachers educate themselves on proper methods of searching on the Internet and develop exercises that teach their students proper Internet search methods and ways to evaluate the credibility of sites. The search engine Google uses automatic filters to increase the likelihood of finding appropriate results, and its methods have proven so successful that other search engines (Yahoo! for example) are licensing the methods.

Older students can also learn to use Boolean searches. With a Boolean search, searchers limit the potential matches by putting quotation marks around key words, using + and - symbols, and adding terms like *and*, *or*, and *not*. For example, simply typing "save the whale organization" in the search window can produce over 100,000 potential matches, using some search engines. Using a Boolean search of the terms *free and whale and organization not animal not sperm not turtles* reduces the offerings to a manageable 122 sites.

If you would like more information about Boolean searches, see the subheading "Boolean search methods" in the Appendix, under "Popular Search Engines," page 139.

teacher tips

For more resources and information about using the computer in the classroom, see the following items in the Appendix:

- Internet Terms
- Online Writing Labs
- Interactive Lessons
- Popular Search Engines
- Useful Online References

NETIQUETTE

Young students should never be "searching" the web without some guidelines. (For very young students, it is best to choose the search engine that they can use and the key words with which they search. It is a good idea to test the searches yourself first. Some seemingly harmless words can bring up appalling results.)

The more control you have over an Internet activity, the less the likelihood of unwelcome surprises. Here are some more suggestions for classroom use of the Internet:

- **Monitor and establish guidelines** for use of the Internet. Make sure that students are familiar with the guidelines.

- **Position computer monitors so screens are visible from a central area.** Try to place them so that they are easily viewed by anyone in a frequent traffic area.

- **Use filtering software on middle and elementary school computers.** The teachers and/or parents should determine which filters to use. Some examples are We-blocker, Cyber Patrol, Net Nanny, and Cybersitter.

- **Distribute and discuss rules for safe use** of the Internet. (Free copies of "Kids' Rules for Online Safety," adapted from the brochure "Child Safety on the Information Highway," by *SafeKids.Com* founder Larry Magid, are available by calling 1-800-843-5678.)

- **Check out any web sites you recommend** to students before you recommend them.

- **Ask students frequently about how they use the Internet** and what sites they visit.

- **Examine students' Internet activities** by looking at the browser history on the computers used. An easy method is to click on "History" (the sundial icon) on a computer's browser toolbar and then select the present day, the past week, or some other period of time. A list of web sites visited on that computer will appear. Another method of checking is to look at the "Cookies" folder on the computer's C drive. There you will see a list of files with the embedded names of web sites that have been visited on the computer. For example, if you find the file *user@seaworld.txt*, someone used the computer to visit *www.seaworld.com*. Such monitoring is not an invasion of privacy where child safety is concerned.

ACTIVITIES

FOR THE

COMPUTER LAB

Word processing programs have been a lifesaver to students and teachers alike, making it far easier to produce a polished piece of work. However, the computer has uses in the language arts classroom that go far beyond simple word processing. The activities that follow use the computer or the computer lab as an integral part of the learning process.

- The activities can be used with either PCs or Macs in any computer lab, using any word processing program.

- Tips for completing a task in Microsoft Word are sometimes included in parentheses. Often these tips are useful for other programs as well and can help point students in the right direction, even if they don't use Microsoft Word.

- *Plugged In to English* presumes that students have some knowledge of basic computer functions, such as opening a file, highlighting, using a mouse, etc.

- Some activities involve the use of the Internet.

- The *Plugged In to English CD-ROM* includes the student instructions to all activities in .pdf format, special text files necessary for some activities, and examples. These files may be accessed from a server, copied to individual computers, or printed out. (Permission is granted to reproduce these items for the purchaser's own classes, so long as the copyright notice is included.)

With "Puzzling a Poem," students study scrambled versions of poems by A.E. Housman and William Blake. Then they unscramble the poems, which both employ couplets. The trick is to recognize the rhymes and reunite the lines. A sense of order develops when the lines are arranged correctly.

The exercise helps students see that poems have a logical pattern of development. Students also gain a better understanding of the role that couplets can play in emphasizing particular ideas and in unifying the poem.

Students will need to open the file "Scrambled Poems" from the *Plugged In to English CD-ROM* included with this book. Be ready to tell them how to access the file. Then they can proceed on their own, following the student instructions on page 29.

A POISON TREE *by William Blake*

Original	Scrambled
I was angry with my friend:	And my foe beheld it shine,
I told my wrath, my wrath did end.	I told it not, my wrath did grow.
I was angry with my foe:	I told my wrath, my wrath did end.
I told it not, my wrath did grow.	And I water'd it in fears,
And I water'd it in fears,	And I sunned it with my smiles,
Night and morning with my tears;	Night and morning with my tears;
And I sunned it with my smiles,	And with soft deceitful wiles.
And with soft deceitful wiles.	And into my garden stole
And it grew both day and night,	I was angry with my friend:
Till it bore an apple bright;	When the night had veil'd the pole:
And my foe beheld it shine,	In the morning glad I see
And he knew that it was mine,	My foe outstretched beneath the tree.
And into my garden stole	I was angry with my foe:
When the night had veil'd the pole:	And it grew both day and night,
In the morning glad I see	Till it bore an apple bright;
My foe outstretched beneath the tree.	And he knew that it was mine,

LOVELIEST OF TREES, THE CHERRY NOW *by A.E. Housman*

Original

Loveliest of trees, the cherry now
Is hung with bloom along the bough,
And stands about the woodland ride
Wearing white for Eastertide.

Now, of my threescore years and ten,
Twenty will not come again,
And take from seventy springs a score,
It only leaves me fifty more.

And since to look at things in bloom
Fifty springs are little room,
About the woodlands I will go
To see the cherry hung with snow.

Scrambled

To see the cherry hung with snow.
Twenty will not come again.
And stands about the woodland ride
Fifty springs are little room
Loveliest of trees, the cherry now
It only leaves me fifty more.
And take from seventy springs a score
About the woodlands I will go
Now, of my threescore years and ten,
Is hung with bloom along the bough,
And since to look at things in bloom
Wearing white for Eastertide.

analyzing poetry

Puzzling a Poem

Poems have a logical pattern of development. The challenge of "Puzzling a Poem" is to unscramble a poem by a well-known author and discover the organizational pattern behind the ideas presented.

Step 1. Open the file entitled "Scrambled Poems." (Your teacher will tell you where to find the file.) Read the scrambled poems.

Step 2. Choose one of the scrambled poems. Open a new document and Copy this poem into it. Put your name, class, and date in the upper right-hand corner of the paper. Then Save the new document as "Puzzling a Poem."

Step 3. Now start rearranging the lines of the poem, trying to determine the original order the author was likely to have used.

(*To copy and paste lines quickly, try using* Ctrl + c *to copy highlighted material. Move your cursor to the position where you wish to paste, and press* Ctrl + v *to paste.*)

Step 4. After you have developed a version of the poem that you are satisfied with, Save it again. Then title the poem. What word or phrase do you think the original poet might have used? Use that word or phrase as your title.

Step 5. Being as specific as possible, write a paragraph that explains the reasons you arranged the lines as you did. Perhaps the best way to explain is to analyze the thought process you followed. What did you do first? What did you try next? Why did you decide one line should go before another?

Step 6. When you are finished, proofread your work. Save it again. Print two copies, and turn in one.

Internet Poems

Involving students in a creative process can often help them become more comfortable reading and responding to poetry. "Internet Poems" should reduce any tensions students might have about the impenetrability of poetry.

In this activity, students work in teams, searching for colorful words, phrases, headlines, advertisements, etc. in web sites they locate on the Internet. To focus their searches, have them choose from the list of topics, below. (Note that the topics are general ones. Students can narrow them to fit their own interests.)

- Graffiti
- Violence
- Desserts
- Children
- Sports
- Education
- Emotions
- Travel
- Famous People
- Animals

Rivers

As students identify colorful words and phrases on their topic, they copy and paste the passages into a document. As they search for words and phrases that evoke and/or convey powerful images, they will develop a fuller understanding and appreciation of the descriptive nature of language. After students have created their lists, they work in teams to create a poem from the words and phrases they have selected.

Having students work in teams works well for several reasons. Some students are already very experienced in searching for information on the Internet, so they can serve as advisors or leaders in this activity. Others can be helpful when paired with concrete thinkers who may have difficulty recognizing the imagistic nature of some words and phrases. Usually a team of two or three results in a good mix of types.

As students work, they should record the web addresses (URLs) of the sites from which they have copied words and phrases. In doing so, they will create a web site report, following the format of the sample report on page 33. Keeping a record of the web addresses is an initial step in documenting information taken from the Internet. When a team turns in the finished version of its Internet poem, it will attach a web site report that includes a complete listing of the Internet sites used, along with the exact words or phrases copied from each.

Special Notes:

- You will need to divide students into small groups of two or three.

- Each group will need a computer station with Internet access.

- Before you start, review some of the images students have encountered in recently discussed poems. For example, if the class has just discussed Dylan Thomas's "Especially when the October Wind," point out these powerful images:

  when the October wind with frosty fingers punishes my hair

  Caught by the crabbing sun I walk on fire

  Hearing the raven cough in winter sticks

  hear the dark-vowelled birds

  Ask students to look for comparable images and phrases that appeal to one of the five senses: sight, sound, touch, taste, and smell.

- Free verse is generally the best poetry form to use in this exercise, though rhymed poetry can also be used.

- Students will be working with a theme. You may assign the general themes and allow students to narrow them to select their own theme topic. Or, depending upon the grade level of students and their experience with poetry, you may want to assign a different theme topic to each group.

- Make certain students take turns, within their groups, searching for and arranging words and phrases. Don't let one member of the team do all the work.

Internet Poems

Have you ever participated in a scavenger hunt? If you have, then you know how much fun one can be. With "Internet Poems," you will be participating in a kind of Internet scavenger hunt. You will be searching for colorful words, phrases, and even whole sentences on a particular topic. You will eventually weave the words together into a free verse poem.

As you copy and paste words, phrases, or lines into a new document, you will also be keeping track of the web sites you have visited.

Step 1. Open a new document in your word processing program and Save it as "Internet Words and Phrases." Then minimize the document and log on to the Internet.

Step 2. Your teacher has assigned a broad, general theme for your Internet poem. Narrow the theme to a very specific topic. For example, if you have been given the theme "food," you might narrow it to "the pleasures of eating ice cream."

Step 3. Select a search engine (Yahoo, Google, Altavista, etc.) Then search for key terms on your topic. For example, if your topic is "the pleasures of eating ice cream," you might use that phrase, in quotation marks, as your search term. Other phrases that you might use would be "ice cream treats," "eating ice cream," "ice cream stories," etc. All of these would generate a list of web sites that you could visit.

Step 4. As you look through different web sites, search for interesting, dynamic, colorful, powerful, figurative, and image-laden words and phrases. For example, in a quick search on the topic "the pleasures of eating ice cream," a team found these terms:

- *emperor of ice cream*
- *bars, sticks, and cones*
- *a whimsical mix*
- *What are a few calories measured against one of life's great pleasures?*
- *pleasures — either immoral, illegal, or fattening.*

Look for words and phrases that appeal to one of the five senses: sight, sound, touch, taste, and smell. Look for words and phrases that create vivid pictures or images in your mind. Look for words and phrases that use interesting words, or combine words in interesting ways.

Step 5. When you find interesting words and phrases, Copy and Paste them into your "Internet Words and Phrases" document. Also Copy and Paste the web address (URL) of each site you are taking information from. To copy a web address, simply highlight the web address in the location bar at the top of the web site and hit Ctrl + c for Copy. Then switch, or toggle, to your document and hit Ctrl + v for Paste. The web address will be pasted into your document. Paste the web address directly under the words and phrases you are copying.

(To toggle in Microsoft Word, choose Window. *A list of the Microsoft Word documents that you have open will appear. Select the document you want to see. In later versions of Word, the titles of the various documents appear at the bottom of the screen. Simply click on whichever document you want to appear on the screen.)*

Your final document should look something like the following example:

SAMPLE "INTERNET WORDS AND PHRASES" DOCUMENT #1

Team Members: Jessica Martinez, Ben Hubert, Maddie Monet, LaTawna Stockley

Topic: The Pleasures of Eating Ice Cream

Phrases copied, with web addresses:

Jake's Ice Creams & Sorbets
http://atlanta.creativeloafing.com/2001-09-19/oral_critic26.html

"Emperor of Ice-Cream"
http://www.burstnet.com/cgi-bin/ads/ba6374a.cgi/7708/RETURN-CODE

Bars, sticks and cones
http://www.fas.usda.gov/info/agexporter/1999/perfectl.html

A whimsical mix
gourmet pleasure
http://www.worldatmydoor.com/sitePage.asp?site_id=1425&Page_number

What are a few calories measured against one of life's great pleasures?
Pleasures — either illegal, immoral or fattening
http://www.azcentral.com/rep/best2000/food/articles/0917icecream.html

Step 6. Because you are part of a team, take turns choosing, copying, and pasting, perhaps switching every two sites. Each time you Copy information and Paste it into your document, be sure to Save.

Step 7. When you think you have enough words and phrases to create a poem, Save again. Print a copy of the document for each member of your team.

writing poetry

Step 8. Now you are ready to *find* the poem in the text you have saved. Each team member should independently review the list, underlining the words and/or phrases he or she thinks should be a part of the poem. So that each team member is clear about what words or phrases should come first, it is a good idea to put a number in front of each copied word or phrase to indicate the order each of you has decided on.

Step 9. Now it is time to create a poem, as a team. Discuss with your other team members your choices and ideas about how the words/phrases should be organized.

You will have to decide whether you are going to write a free verse poem or a rhymed one. A rhymed poem will take more time and require you to add additional words or phrases to develop your rhyme and meter. A free verse poem does not have to rhyme, though it usually has an established meter or line pattern.

Look at the following examples of the start of poems on the topic "the pleasures of eating ice cream."

SAMPLE INTERNET POEM
RHYMED

The Pleasures of Eating Ice Cream

A whimsical mix of gourmet pleasure
Often shaped in bars, sticks, and cones
Isn't illegal or immoral but a treasure
That doesn't add muscle to bones.

SAMPLE INTERNET POEM
FREE VERSE

The Pleasures of Eating Ice Cream

What are a few calories
When it involves a whimsical mix?
No matter the shape —
Bars, sticks, and cones —
Ice cream is one of life's great pleasures.

Note that in both versions, whether rhymed or free verse, words and punctuation have been added. The trick is first figuring out the order of the words and phrases you want to use and then filling in with connective tissue – your own words and punctuation – to make the lines flow. Don't be afraid to drop articles such as *a*, *an*, and *the*. Try to keep your phrasing tight and economical. Let your ideas reveal themselves through key words and images. (For another example of a web site report, see below. For another example of an Internet poem, see page 36.)

Step 10. Once you have made decisions as a team about the narrative and/or descriptive order of your words and phrases, you are ready to begin structuring your

SAMPLE "INTERNET WORDS AND PHRASES" DOCUMENT #2

Team Members: Lee Benham, Rajani Thankar, Max Holtzer, Sam Prust

Poem Topic: Graffiti

Phrases copied, with web addresses:

Art Crimes: The Writing on the Wall

> *http://www.graffiti.org/*

A special form of communication

> *http://www.inigraphics.net/publications/topics/2003/issue1/1_03a12.pdf*

ability to transfer what they are feeling / they are able to make it into something beautiful

> *http://www.sarasota.k12.fl.us/bhs/bryan/bryan_grafcg.html*

decipher it bit by bit, and all of a sudden you're able to get meaning out of it

> *http://www.dailybruin.ucla.edu/db/issues/99/10.19/ae.bookzone.html*

colors and swirls

> *http://www.abstraktkonfusionrecords.com/graffhistory.html*

encourage this aerosol art culture via public murals and legal graffiti spaces

> *http://home.vicnet.net.au/~artsalive/cues/Cue12-02.rtf*

Through the seventies and eighties creativity peaked in the subways of New York as writers bombed carts with reckless abandon

> *http://www.jhblive.co.za/writers/features/grafity/default.htm*

intricate and complex

> *http://www.taxionline.com/nine/graff1.html*

bomb, tag, fade

> *http://www.b-boys.com/graffitivocab.html*

SAMPLE INTERNET POEM #2

Graffiti

Wall covered in colors and swirls;
Bomb, tag, fade.
A special form of communication
Peaked in the subways of New York.
It may be illegal,
But some encourage this aerosol art
Via public murals and legal spaces.

Intricate and complex,
It is possible to decipher it bit by bit.
It is the ability to transfer what they are
feeling;
They are able to make it into something
beautiful.

---

final poem. Open another document in your word processing program and Save it as "Internet Poem." Copy and Paste the words and phrases you have chosen for your poem, in the order chosen, into the document. Delete unwanted material. Add the words and punctuation you have selected. When you are finished, title your work, choosing a significant word or phrase from the body of the poem. Save your work.

Step 11. Print copies of your final "Internet Poem" for each member of your group. Print two more copies, one to turn in and one for the class poetry anthology.

Step 12. Print a copy of your original list of "Internet Words and Phrases." Add a copy of the final "Internet Poem," and staple both documents together, to turn in.

Converting an element of a short story into poetry is a challenging but effective way for students to exercise their creativity. As a side benefit, they may gain a better understanding of some of the differences between the two genres. With "Character Poem," students create a poem about a character in a short story they have read.

Special Notes:

- You will need to divide students into groups of two or three. One of the students will be responsible for the group's typing.

- Assign each group a short story to read before they begin the activity. All groups can use the same short story, or you can assign different stories to different groups.

Alternative Activity:

An alternative or follow-up assignment is to have students select their own stories and repeat the exercise, this time working individually.

Character Poem

"Character Poem" challenges you to convert one element of a short story, character development, into poetic form. In the computer lab, your team will create a poem that is a portrait of one of the major characters in the story.

Homework

You have been appointed to a team of two and assigned a story. You are to read the story and analyze it before coming to the computer lab. Here are some questions to consider:

- What are the most powerful passages? Which ones describe characters in the story?

- What metaphors and other figures of speech can you identify? Which ones relate to characters in the story?

- What are the major themes of the story? What parts do the major characters play in helping develop those themes?

Step 1. Select a team captain. Choose the best typist to be captain, as he or she will enter the words and phrases the team members think of. To write the poem, you will need to work together at the computer.

Step 2. Open a new file and Save it as, "Character Notes."

Step 3. Choose one of the main characters in your short story as the subject of your poem. Use the following questions to develop images and figurative language about the character you have selected. Use strong verbs and concrete nouns in your answers. Record these ideas in your document.

- How should you refer to the character? Should you use his or her name or nickname? Or is it best to refer to this character as "son," "sister," "the other one," or some such reference?

- What strong verbs characterize his/her movements: walk, gestures, posture, etc.?

- What animal or object does he/she most resemble?

- What color are his/her eyes, hair, skin? Can they be compared to anything?

- What does your character most fear, hate, love?

- Does he/she have any unique mannerisms? Describe them.

- What are his/her ambitions, dreams?

- In what place would you most likely find this person? Describe the place.

- What is your character doing there?

- Is this character best presented alone or with others?

Answering these questions will probably help you think of other information about your character. Write down any other information about your character that you think is relevant.

Step 4. Once you have answered your questions, decide on the form your poem will take. Will it be a free verse poem? Or will it have a set line length and rhyme? (Because your time in the lab is limited, your best option is probably free verse.)

Step 5. When your team is ready to draft a poem, Open a new document and Save it as "Character Poem." (Keep your "Character Notes" document open. You can move back and forth, or toggle, between the two documents.)

(To toggle in Microsoft Word, choose Window. A list of the Microsoft Word documents that you have open will appear. Select the document you want to see. In later versions of Word, the titles of the various documents appear at the bottom of the screen. Simply click on whichever document you want to appear on the screen.)

Step 6. Toggle to your "Character Poem" document. With your partner, "freewrite" a poem about the character you have selected. To freewrite, simply let your thoughts flow, and record them as fast as you can.

Step 7. Let your feelings at the time the words appear on the page determine what length the line should be. Hit Enter whenever you feel it's time to move to the next line.

Step 8. Keep looking at your "Character Notes" for ideas. You can even Copy and Paste phrases from your list into your new creation, to save time.

Step 9. When you have all your ideas down, go back over the rough draft of your poem. How can you improve it? Should you take out certain phrases? Add more detail? Move things around? Polish and proofread your poem as much as you can in the time allowed.

Step 10. Choose a title and insert it at the beginning of your poem. Remember that a title should be descriptive and definitive. You might want to look for a key phrase in the poem and use it as a title.

Step 11. Now Save and Print enough copies for all team members and the teacher, plus a copy to share with another team.

Homework

Exchange your poem with another team. Read that team's poem, and then write at least two paragraphs explaining whether or not that team's poem effectively captures the essence of the character selected.

Two Thumbs Up

Everyone is a critic, and students are no exception. They like to offer their opinions on TV shows, movies, sporting events, and many other subjects. Why not stories that they read?

"Two Thumbs Up" invites students to use an approach made famous by the movie critics Gene Siskel and Roger Ebert on the former television show *Siskel and Ebert*. Students today may be more familiar with *At the Movies*, which features Roger Ebert and a new critic, Richard Roeper.

To introduce the exercise, you might play an audio of an "Ebert and Roeper" discussion of a contemporary film. (The audios are available, as of this writing, at *http://tvplex.go.com/buenavista/ebertandroeper/video.html*.) Emphasize that the Ebert and Roeper reviews have the following characteristics:

- a conversational tone
- a brief identification of the work being reviewed
- a concise summary of the plot and then of the work
- a discussion of the merits and weaknesses of the work, supported by quick references to specific scenes
- a recommendation to the audience about the quality of the work (Each reviewer gives a "thumbs up" or a "thumbs down.")

After the discussion, have students proceed on their own, following the student instructions on page 41. They will be writing a review of a short story, in Siskel and Roeper style.

Special Notes:

- Students will need to work in pairs.
- Students must read a short story before they can begin the activity. Any short story will work.

Two Thumbs Up

Everyone likes to offer an opinion. Here's your chance to give a "thumbs up" or a "thumbs down" to a short story, using an approach from a television show you may be familiar with: *At the Movies*. In the show, Roger Ebert and Richard Roeper each give a "thumbs up" or a "thumbs down" to movies they have screened.

You have been paired with another classmate and given a short story to read. Before your next computer lab, you and your partner should read the story, paying attention to its theme, plots and subplots, setting, style, and characters. Take notes to bring to class.

In class, you and your partner will write a review of the short story, in dialogue form.

Step 1. Open a new document and Save it as "Two Thumbs Up." Put your names, class, and date in the upper right-hand corner of the paper.

Step 2. Decide who will be the typist. Real teamwork is needed to make this exercise run smoothly. If one of you is a better typist, then that person can do all the typing. The other can simply dictate his or her lines. Another idea is to take turns typing.

Step 3. Now you will write a review of the short story you have read, using a dialogue format, like a play. One of you should start your review by introducing the work being discussed. The other should then briefly summarize the story.

Step 4. Next, develop a conversation or dialogue between the two of you that reflects each of your opinions about the story. Be certain to use passages from the story to illustrate or explain your ideas about the merits and weaknesses of the piece. Here's an example:

SAMPLE DIALOGUE

Ebert: Last night I read a short story entitled "A Rose for Emily," by Pulitzer prize-winning American author William Faulkner.

Roeper: I did, too. The plot of the story is quite simple. One of the citizens in the little Southern town where she lives tells us about Miss Emily, a spinster woman whose father discourages suitors.

Ebert: Yes, when I started reading it, I thought it was going to be really boring, but I soon found myself caught up in the story.

Roeper: I felt the same way — bored, that is — until the part in the story where they find a grey hair in the indentation on the pillow next to a corpse in Emily's house. Then I was unable to stop reading.

When you develop your dialogue, you can stay with the names Ebert and Roeper, use fictional names, or use your own names.

Step 5. As you type in your team's comments, be sure to support your points. Ebert and Roeper don't trounce a film or applaud a film without providing detailed explanations of its strengths and weaknesses. Follow their lead as you review your short story. Perhaps the plot is so simple or trite it doesn't grab your interest. You might write something along these lines:

SAMPLE DIALOGUE

Ebert: Yes, when I started reading it, I thought the plot wasn't complicated enough. I mean, who wants to read about an old woman who never married the man she loved because her father didn't approve of him?

Roeper: I felt the same way, but then when I found out that . . .

Ebert and Roeper don't always agree. You don't have to either. Your task is to write a developed, thoughtful review of the story you both have read. Have fun!

Step 6. When you finish your dialogue, proofread and Save. Then Print three copies, one for each of the reviewers and one for your teacher.

With "Literary Résumés," students create a résumé for a character in a novel they have just read. The activity is a playful but practical way for students to hone their character analysis skills.

It is a good idea to collect a few résumés and bring them to the lab the day of the exercise. Pass them around for students to examine. They may also look at the examples on pages 45-47 and on the *Plugged In to English CD-ROM*.

Résumé Templates

Most word processing programs, such as *Microsoft Word*, have templates or wizards that aid students in creating résumés. Look under your Help menu to determine if your word processing program has these features. Students who learn to use templates can find them useful for a variety of other purposes.

Résumé templates and wizards can lighten the workload for your students, but they are not absolutely necessary for completing this activity. If you do not have access to a résumé template, students can create résumés by copying the format of one of the example résumés brought to class.

Literary Résumés

With "Literary Résumés," you will be developing a résumé for a character from the novel you have just read. Use your imagination to create your literary résumé!

Step 1. Choose the character you want to write about. Jot down notes about the character: name, age, address, education, work experience, etc. If there is nothing in the literary work that applies to a specific category, then imagine how that character *might* fill out the résumé.

Try to "become" the character in your mind. Imagine. Role play. Some information appropriate for each part of the résumé should come to you.

Step 2. Go to your word processing program's résumé template or wizard.

(In Microsoft Word, find the résumé templates under the File menu, New. Depending upon the version of Microsoft Word you are using, click next on either Other Documents or More Word Templates or Office 97 Templates. A list of résumé templates should appear.)

Step 3. Select the résumé format you want to use. When the template is displayed on the screen, Save it as "Literary Résumé".

(The example on page 45 was done in Microsoft Word using the Elegant Résumés template.)

Step 4. Begin replacing the information in the template with the information about your literary character. To do this, highlight the words you wish to replace. Do not click or delete. Just begin typing in the words that you are substituting. The words will fall automatically into the section you have highlighted.

Step 5. When you finish, proofread the résumé, Save it, and Print two copies. Turn one in to your teacher.

SAMPLE RÉSUMÉ [elegant template]

JACK MERRIDEW
(Lord of the Flies)

OBJECTIVE

To establish myself as leader of a tribe noted for hunting prowess.

EXPERIENCE

WWII, Britain
Choir Leader of a private boys' school
■ Unified and led a boys' choir.
■ Won the Boys' School Best Choir Award.

After Plane Crash
Chief of pig hunters
■ Controlled the conch.
■ Established pig-roasting fires around the island.

EDUCATION

1941 to present
■ Private British Boys' School
■ Pacific Island School of Hard Knocks

INTERESTS

■ Thwarting Ralph and his followers Piggy, Simon, and the Samneric twins
■ Hunting pigs and roaming the island

MOST SIGNICANT ACHIEVEMENT

Slaying of the pig and creating the "Lord of the Flies" from its head.

**CONCH SIGNAL: THREE RAPID NOTES
FORT CASTLE ROCK, PACIFIC ISLAND**

analyzing characters

SAMPLE RÉSUMÉ (contemporary template)

Mill Road, Lowell, Massachusetts   (123) 456-7890
Lyddie@theweavingroom.com

Lyddie

(*Lyddie*), by Katherine Patterson

Objective

To obtain secure employment to buy back the farm.

Experience

Daughter
- Helped run the farm after Pa left.
- Saved the family from the bear.
- Sold the cow to the Stevens.

Maid
- Did the washing and the cleaning up at Cutler's Tavern.
- Worked from sunup to sundown, and then some.
- Befriended Triphina.

Mill Girl
- Tended four looms at once.
- Trained Brigid.
- Was considered Mr. Marsden's "best girl."
- Fired for "moral turpitude."

Education
- Learned to read and write from Diana.
- Read Charles Dickens' *Oliver Twist* and know most passages by heart.
- Taught Brigid how to read.

Interests

Earning money, taking care of Rachel, Luke Stevens.

SAMPLE RÉSUMÉ (professional template)

123 Love Road, Elsewhere 12345-6789

PHONE: (123) 987-6543
FAX: (123) 456-7890
E-MAIl: jonas@elsewhere.com

Jonas (The Giver)

Objective

To save Gabriel from "release"

Experience

Receiver of Memory   The community

• Received memories of courage and bravery.

• Working knowledge of the world before the implementation
• of climate control.

• Previous experience in helping Gabriel sleep peacefully.
• Watched the release of the twin.

Escapee   Elsewhere

• Evaded capture by recalling memories of cold when heat-seeking planes were overhead.

• Helping transfer memories of warmth to Gabe.

• Intuitively knew location of sled during blizzard.

Education

• Achieved Ceremony of Twelve.

• Performed requisite volunteer hours.

• Learned about *"back and back and back"* from the Giver.

Interests

The color red, helping Gabe, love

Most Significant Achievement

Escaping to *Elsewhere* with Gabriel.

Putting It in Order

"Putting It in Order" gives students practice organizing in a sequential manner. First, they open up a scrambled version of Jack London's account in *Colliers* magazine of the May 5, 1906, earthquake in San Francisco. By cutting and pasting within a saved version of the document, they try to reconstruct the paragraph in its original order. Then they check how well they did by logging onto an Internet site containing the original version.

Next, they open up a scrambled version of a three-paragraph excerpt from *War of the Worlds*, by H.G. Wells. Again, they unscramble and then check how well they did. In both cases they write about their organizational observations.

SAN FRANCISCO EARTHQUAKE *by Jack London*

Scrambled

1. And for three days and nights this lurid tower swayed in the sky, reddening the sun, darkening the day, and filling the land with smoke.
2. But the conflagration that followed burned up hundreds of millions of dollars' worth of property.
3. Its social and residential section is wiped out.
4. Not in history has a modern imperial city been so completely destroyed. San Francisco is gone.
5. There is no estimating within hundreds of millions the actual damage wrought.
6. Its industrial section is wiped out.
7. Nothing remains of it but memories and a fringe of dwelling-houses on its outskirts.
8. The earthquake shook down in San Francisco hundreds of thousands of dollars worth of walls and chimneys.
9. The factories and warehouses, the great stores and newspaper buildings, the hotels and the palaces of the nabobs, are all gone.
10. Within an hour after the earthquake shock, the smoke of San Francisco's burning was a lurid tower visible a hundred miles away.
11. Its business section is wiped out.
12. Remains only the fringe of dwelling houses on the outskirts of what was once San Francisco.

Original

The earthquake shook down in San Francisco hundreds of thousands of dollars worth of walls and chimneys. But the conflagration that followed burned up hundreds of millions of dollars' worth of property. There is no estimating within hundreds of millions the actual damage wrought. Not in history has a modern imperial city been so completely destroyed. San Francisco is gone. Nothing remains of it but memories and a fringe of dwelling-houses on its outskirts. Its industrial section is wiped out. Its business section is wiped out. Its social and residential section is wiped out. The factories and warehouses, the great stores and newspaper buildings, the hotels and the palaces of the nabobs, are all gone. Remains only the fringe of dwelling houses on the outskirts of what was once San Francisco.

organizing sequentially

WAR OF THE WORLDS *by H.G. Wells*

Scrambled

1. His shoulders were hunched, so that his head was hidden from me.
2. I whispered for the curate several times, and at last felt my way to the door of the kitchen.
3. After eating we crept back to the scullery, and there I must have dozed again, for when presently I looked round I was alone.
4. It was still daylight, and I perceived him across the room, lying against the triangular hole that looked out upon the Martians.
5. The thudding vibration continued with wearisome persistence.

1. For a minute or so I remained watching the curate, and then I advanced, crouching and stepping with extreme care amid the broken crockery that littered the floor.
2. Through the aperture in the wall I could see the top of a tree touched with gold and the warm blue of a tranquil evening sky.
3. I could hear a number of noises almost like those in an engine shed; and the place rocked with that beating thud.

1. The detachment of the plaster had left a vertical slit open in the debris, and by raising myself cautiously across a beam I was able to see out of this gap into what had been overnight a quiet suburban roadway.
2. Then I turned to see how much of our rampart remained.
3. Vast, indeed, was the change that we beheld.
4. I touched the curate's leg, and he started so violently that a mass of plaster went sliding down outside and fell with a loud impact.
5. I gripped his arm, fearing he might cry out, and for a long time we crouched motionless.

Original

After eating we crept back to the scullery, and there I must have dozed again, for when presently I looked round I was alone. The thudding vibration continued with wearisome persistence. I whispered for the curate several times, and at last felt my way to the door of the kitchen. It was still daylight, and I perceived him across the room, lying against the triangular hole that looked out upon the Martians. His shoulders were hunched, so that his head was hidden from me.

I could hear a number of noises almost like those in an engine shed; and the place rocked with that beating thud. Through the aperture in the wall I could see the top of a tree touched with gold and the warm blue of a tranquil evening sky. For a minute or so I remained watching the curate, and then I advanced, crouching and stepping with extreme care amid the broken crockery that littered the floor.

I touched the curate's leg, and he started so violently that a mass of plaster went sliding down outside and fell with a loud impact. I gripped his arm, fearing he might cry out, and for a long time we crouched motionless. Then I turned to see how much of our rampart remained. The detachment of the plaster had left a vertical slit open in the debris, and by raising myself cautiously across a beam I was able to see out of this gap into what had been overnight a quiet suburban roadway. Vast, indeed, was the change that we beheld.

Putting It in Order

When you are revising an informative paper, make sure that you give facts in an organized way. "Putting It in Order" will give you practice organizing information. Note that there are two parts to the exercise.

Part I

Step 1. Open the file "London Scrambled." Your teacher will tell you where to find it. The file contains the first paragraph from Jack London's famous *Colliers* magazine account of the May 5, 1906, earthquake in San Francisco. However, the sentences of the original paragraph have been rearranged. Save the file you have opened as "London Unscrambled."

Step 2. Begin to Cut and Paste the different lines, trying to arrange them the way you think London did. Keep rearranging until you have a version that you think is sensible, clear and organized. When you think you have the right arrangement, Save it. Then compare your version with London's original. (Your teacher will tell you where to find it.)

Step 3. Once you have studied the original version, add a paragraph or two under your version of London's work. First describe how he organized the original. Then explain how well you did at unscrambling.

Step 4. Save. Print out two copies and turn in one.

Part II

Step 1. Open the file, "H.G. Wells Scrambled." The file contains three paragraphs from the famous 19th century novel, *War of the Worlds*, by H.G. Wells. Save it as "H.G. Wells Unscrambled."

Step 2. Repeat Steps 2, above, with this new material.

Step 3. When you think you have the right arrangement, Save it. Then compare your version with Wells's original. (Your teacher will tell you where to find it.)

Step 4. Once you have studied the original version, add a paragraph or two under your version of Wells's work. First describe how he organized the original. Then explain how well you did at unscrambling.

Step 5. Save. Print out two copies and turn in one.

organizing sequentially

Are you tired of the traditional character sketches you have students write? Want to whet their appetites to read other literary works? Or are you looking for additional activities for literature circles you have established? If so, have your students try "Wanted Posters."

As you will see once you assign them, students will have a great deal of fun creating wanted posters, and the finished products will attract a great deal of attention. They can be displayed in the classroom and throughout the school to entice others to read the literary works.

If you have access to a color printer, be sure to give students the opportunity to print their creations in full color. Even if you don't have a color printer, many students will have access to one at home.

Wanted Poster

Wanted Posters

Think about the "Wanted" posters you see at the post office, or the "Wanted: Dead or Alive" flyers you see in old Western movies. You are going to create a similar kind of poster based on a character from literature.

Step 1. Choose a villain from a literary work you have read – a novel, a poem, a play, a short story. On paper, sketch out a design for a "Wanted" poster based on this character. A "Wanted" poster usually includes the word "Wanted" across the top of the poster, with a face under it. For this poster, you will also want space for a paragraph describing what the villain has done.

Step 2. Open a new document and Save it as "Wanted Poster." Type in your heading and center it. Highlight the heading and choose an appropriate font style and size. You will probably want to select Bold as well. Be sure to include in the heading the villain's name and anything else that would help identify him/her. Here's an example:

WANTED:
JACK, LEADER OF SAVAGE BOYS
MAROONED ON THE ISLAND
IN *LORD OF THE FLIES*

Step 3. Choose a background color for your poster.

(In Microsoft Word, choose Format, *then* Background. *Make your selection from the color palate that appears.)*

Step 4. Type in a paragraph or two explaining *why* this villain is wanted. What evil deed has he/she committed? Why is he/she a villain? Be as specific as possible.

Step 5. Now it's time to insert a picture of your villain. Choose a drawing from your word processor's clip art file. Or, choose a photograph from another source. (You could scan a photograph and save it as a file, use a photograph taken with a digital camera, or insert a photograph from an on-line source of free photographs, like *www.foto4.com* or *www.freestockphotos.com*.

(To insert Clip Art *in Microsoft Word, choose* Insert, *then* Picture, *then* Clip Art. *Then select a drawing — or in later versions of Word, choose a category and then a drawing.*

To insert a picture or photograph scanned and saved as a file, choose Insert, *then* Picture, *then* From File *instead of* Clip Art. *Choose the location where you have saved the file.)*

Step 6. Insert the clip art or photograph that you have selected. When the picture appears in the document, enlarge it to fill up most of the page.

(In Microsoft Word, click on the picture. Tiny squares and a box will appear to frame the picture. Click your mouse on a corner cube and drag out the corner, making certain the picture enlarges proportionately, until the picture fills up most of the page.)

Step 7. View your poster at a percentage of 25-50%, so that you can see the whole poster at once. Check to see if the picture is the right size and is positioned correctly. Make any adjustments necessary.

*(In Microsoft Word, go to the **Zoom** box on the toolbar. The **Zoom** box is the one that shows a box with a percentage in it. Click on the arrow next to the box and choose a smaller percentage — probably 25-50%.*
*Or click on **View**, then **Zoom**. Under **Percent**, use the arrows to select a percentage.)*

Step 8. Once you have determined that the poster looks the way you want it to and contains all the necessary information about your villain, **Save** your work. **Print** two copies. Write your name, class, and date on the reverse side of the posters. Then turn one in.

SAMPLE WANTED POSTER

WANTED
TYBALT CAPULET

Beware if you meet this man!
The ultimate bad boy, Tybalt Capulet picks a fight with anyone and everyone who crosses his path, including Benvolio, Lord Capulet, Mercutio and Romeo.
He is boiling over with rage and hatred, especially if you are a Montague.

If you encounter this man, call authorities. Do not approach.
Gruff and hot-tempered, he prefers wielding a sword to holding a conversation.
Consider him armed and dangerous.

Computer Chat

Tired of class discussions falling flat because students are reluctant to discuss freely their reactions or interpretations of a work? If so, try "Computer Chat," which creates a mock chat room environment for students to discuss literary works. The anonymity of a chat room draws students out. It is especially effective with quiet students who have excellent insights into the works but are reluctant to share in an open discussion.

The chat room approach can be used for any genre. The first attempt may prove a bit chaotic, but students appreciate the opportunity to present their views without having all eyes focused on them, as is the case in a traditional classroom setting.

After students have had an opportunity to chat about a literary work, have them print out the responses, making enough copies for everyone who used each computer station. Students can then use the comments to help develop an analytical paper on the literature being discussed.

Special Notes

- Base the chat room discussion on three literary works that students have read. Any novel, short story, poem, or play can be used as the basis for discussion.

- To help students focus, you will need to give them a list of questions about each of the three literary works chosen. You can use questions from the text or develop original ones. It's a good idea to limit the number of questions to no more than three so that students have an opportunity to move to several computer stations during the lab period.

- You will need to assign a color to each of the literary works. For example, you might assign yellow to the poem "Miniver Cheevy," printing questions about "Miniver Cheevy" on yellow paper and putting yellow self-stick notes on all the computers where students can chat about "Miniver Cheevy." Everything related to another piece of literature might be colored green, and everything related to yet another might be colored blue.

Computer Chat

With "Computer Chat," you and your classmates will engage in simulated chat room discussions about literary works that you have read.

Each computer station has been color-coded, with one color assigned to each of the three pieces of literature you will be discussing. The steps that follow will guide you through the exercise.

Step 1. You have been given a colored sheet of paper with a list of questions about a particular piece of literature. For this activity, each computer station has been dedicated to a certain piece of literature. Find a computer with a colored tag the same color as your question sheet.

Step 2. At the computer tagged in the same color as your question sheet, Open a new document in your word processing program and Save it as "Computer Chat." Type in a heading at the top of the document: "Computer Chat on _____," filling in the blank with the name of the piece of literature you have been assigned. Center the heading and hit Enter twice.

Step 3. Before answering any of the questions on your colored sheet, choose an alias to use instead of your actual name. Type the name you have selected in Bold. *(Make sure your text is no longer centered.)* Then type your answers to the questions on your colored sheet. You may use your text if you wish to cite specific passages. *(See page 57 for an example of a chat room conversation.)*

Step 4. Be certain to put all your answers under your code name. When you have answered all the questions, Save your work, take your colored slip to the teacher's desk, pick up a question sheet of a different color, and find a computer marked with that color.

Step 5. At the second monitor, read the first person's responses, respond to them, and then write your own responses to the questions. Be sure to type in your alias before you respond.

Step 6. When you are finished, Save your work, pick up a new set of questions, and repeat the process, above. Be sure to respond to questions from all three literary works. If time allows, you may go back to any computer and respond again to what others have written.

Step 7. At the end of lab, count the number of people who have answered the questions at the computer monitor wherever you are. Then Save and Print out enough copies for each person, plus one for the teacher.

Step 8. Turn in one copy and keep one. The remaining copies should be placed at the computer they came from to be picked up by the individuals with the code names printed on the sheet.

EXAMPLE

Computer Chat on "Miniver Cheevy"

Chief says:

Miniver is the kind of guy who lives in the past; he doesn't like the present. I'm not sure why, but he dislikes it enough that he drinks. He also loves money, but he thinks about it more than he works to get it.

(Chief continues with answers to the other questions).

U2 says:

I agree. Miniver is in love with the chivalrous qualities of medieval life. He believes all the legends about knights and their "grace." He is foolish in his beliefs. Otherwise, why would he miss "iron clothing?" A suit of armor was not something pleasant to wear.

(U2 continues with answers to the other questions).

Sir says:

I agree with both of you, but you've missed the real point. Miniver's fascination with the ancient past is just a way for him to escape living in the present. He sees himself as doomed – calls it "fate" – because he was "born too late." His romantic notion of "days of old" is just an excuse to do nothing.

(Sir continues with answers to the other questions.)

responding to literature

Reader's Theater

Students usually enjoy presenting reader's theater scripts. With this exercise, they create their own!

You or your students may select the stories to use, but they should be no more than five or six pages in length. They should also contain a lot of dialogue and have some description of setting. The point of view of the story doesn't matter. Even a first-person narrative such as Sandra Cisneros' "Eleven" can be adapted for several characters. (Remember that if you wish to perform reader's theater outside of the classroom, you will need to select a short story for which the copyright has expired.)

It is a good idea to use stories students have already read. If you decide to use something you haven't discussed in class, be sure students have read the text before you begin this project.

To create the reader's theater scripts, the stories will need to be scanned or typed into a word processing program. The easiest approach, of course, is to scan the stories straight onto the computer with reliable character recognition software. Another approach is to simply have students type the story before you begin this exercise. Students will then adapt the stories to reader's theater by manipulating the original text.

Before you begin, it's a good idea to demonstrate how to develop a script by working from a short story text. First, show your students a copy of a page from a story. Next, highlight dialogue of the various characters and insert name labels to delineate the lines the reader or actor would speak while playing the part. Also, point out that it may be necessary to create a narrator character to provide background or setting information.

This exercise can usually be completed in one or two lab periods. Students can work individually or in small groups.

writing drama

Reader's Theater

If you enjoy films and plays, especially those adapted from popular books such as *Harry Potter and the Sorcerer's Stone* or *Lord of the Rings: Fellowship of the Ring,* you will enjoy reader's theater. It will involve you in a creative process much like that which many scriptwriters follow when they adapt famous books. You will be creating a script that you and your classmates can actually perform as reader's theater.

If you are unfamiliar with reader's theater, think of it as a kind of abridged theater. Actors, usually dressed in dark clothing, sit on chairs and read aloud a play, often a short one-act adapted from a poem or short story. Usually there are no props or special lighting.

Step 1. Scan the story you will be working with into your word processing program, using character recognition software. If you can't scan it, type in the story. Make sure the author's name appears at the beginning of the text. **Save** the file as "Reader's Theater."

Step 2. Now start identifying the different speakers in the story. **Highlight** each speaker's dialogue with a different color, choosing strong colors that will be visible on the screen. That way you will be able to quickly identify who is saying what. For example, all words spoken by a character named Eleanor might be red, and all those spoken by Joshua might be green.

*(In Microsoft Word, you can change the color of your text by using the **Font Color** icon on the toolbar. It looks like an underlined boldface **A** with an arrow tip beside it. **Highlight** the text you wish to make a different color. Click on the **Font Color** icon. It will apply whatever color was most recently used to your text. If you want to apply a different color, click on the arrow to the right of the **Font Color** icon. Select the color you want and click the **Font Color** icon again.)*

Step 3. Continue changing the color of each speaker's text until you have highlighted and colored all the dialogue. **Save** the changes.

Step 4. Now examine the text that remains. What is important to the story? What might be eliminated or communicated in another way? For example, if your leftover text includes a description about an object that is important, perhaps a prop could suggest it. Another idea would be to have one of the characters *tell* its importance. Of course, you would try to make the dialogue sound like something that character would actually say.

If there is still text you must include but it doesn't fit any of your characters, consider creating a narrator to present this information. If you do create a narrator character, make sure to choose a color and highlight text for that speaker as well.

Step 5. **Delete** any text that seems extraneous or unnecessary as part of a play. **Save** the changes.

Step 6. Now you are ready to begin formatting the text as a play. Look at the example below.

EXAMPLE

Original dialogue:

> "You're probably right," my father said. "If we don't act quickly, we will never control it."
> A smile breaking across her face, Mother whispered under her breath, "Thank goodness, he isn't going to turn stubborn again."

Formatted for reader's theater:

Father:	You're probably right. (*Sighing*) If we don't act quickly, we will never control it.
Mother:	(*Smiling and whispering under her breath*) Thank goodness, he isn't going to turn stubborn again.

As the example demonstrates, you need to eliminate quotation marks and use the character's name, followed by a colon, to introduce the dialogue. As you do this, you will eliminate all paragraph indentations characteristic of regular prose fiction. You may also wish to insert, within parentheses, directions as to how the reader is to speak the lines.

To indent the lines that follow the speaker's name, you will need to set up a hanging indent. You might want to consult **Help** for directions for how to create a hanging indent in your program.

*(In Microsoft Word, **Highlight** all the dialogue you wish to format. Click on **Format**, and then choose **Paragraph**. On the first tab, **Indents and Spacing**, go to the section on **Indentation**. Select **Hanging** under the **Special** pull-down menu. Then set the size of the hanging indent under **By**. For play dialogue, it is a good idea to set the indent at 0.25 - 1 inch. After this is set, enter a **Tab** after each character's name. The text should line up. If necessary, repeat the process for each section of dialogue.)*

Step 7. After you have successfully turned all of the text into dialogue, eliminate all the colored highlights and change the entire document into ordinary black text. **Save** the changes.

(In Microsoft Word, choose Edit on the Menu, then Select All. Go to the toolbar and click on the Font Color icon. Click on the color black in the color selection window that opens.)

Step 8. Print a copy of your text and get together with the team or group you have been assigned.

Step 9. In your team or group, examine one another's versions of the script. Which has the most merit? The scripts will probably be similar in many ways, but one person's choice of how to handle parts of the script may be more effective than someone else's. Select one script to present as reader's theater, or combine the best parts of more than one script into one text.

Step 10. After you have read the other versions, you may have ideas for ways to improve your own script. Return to your computer and revise. When you are finished, Print two copies. Turn in one and keep one to share with class members. If your version is chosen for a reader's theater performance, Print enough copies for all readers. Save the changes.

writing drama

Minor Soliloquies

When your students are studying Shakespeare, are they actually reading the plays you assign? Are they paying attention when scenes are read in class? One way to find out — and to encourage them to pay attention — is to have them write a soliloquy for a minor character in a play. How much students understand is quickly revealed when they relate part of the story through a minor character's thoughts.

You might introduce the exercise by telling students about contemporary British playwright Tom Stoppard's play *Rosencrantz and Guildenstern Are Dead*. This sequel to Shakespeare's *Hamlet* focuses on two minor characters who are friends of Hamlet. They are employed by Hamlet's stepfather to kill Hamlet. The play is a philosophical examination of these minor characters and their fate once Hamlet discovers their betrayal.

After a brief review of soliloquies, perhaps sharing a few samples, have students proceed on their own with the student instructions.

Special Notes:

- This activity works well with any Shakespeare play that you may be studying in class.
- You may want to point out that Shakespeare's soliloquies rhyme. For a real challenge you might require students to rhyme their soliloquies as well.

analyzing drama

Minor Soliloquies

You are going to help right an injustice that has rankled many readers of Shakespeare's plays. Because the major characters have all the soliloquies and the long speeches, the minor characters in the plays are often short-changed.

You will correct this injustice by writing a 10-15 line soliloquy for any one of the minor characters in the Shakespeare play you are studying.

Step 1. Choose a minor character from the play. Decide on an observation that character might make about someone else in the play or about something that happens in the play. Take notes about what you might have the character say.

Step 2. Open a new document in your word processing program. Save this document as "Minor Soliloquy." Type your name, class, and date in the upper right-hand corner of the paper.

Step 3. Write your soliloquy, making certain not to tell for which character the soliloquy is being written.

Step 4. When you have finished your soliloquy, Save your file, but leave it open. Exchange computers with another member of the class.

Step 5. Now read the soliloquy on the screen you have just moved to. Decide which character you think is giving the soliloquy.

Step 6. Double space after the soliloquy. Explain who you think is giving the soliloquy, and why. In explaining your reasons, be sure to refer to the character's actions and statements in the play.

Step 7. After you finish your explanation, Save and Print three copies. Keep one, give one to the author of the soliloquy, and turn in one.

Computer Freewriting

When students are stuck for ideas, or when they just need to loosen up a bit, computer freewriting can be a wonderful exercise to get the juices flowing!

The directions given are for unguided freewriting. Another approach is to have students try focused freewriting, starting with a broad, general topic and using the exercise to help them narrow their focus.

prewriting

Computer Freewriting

A great way to generate ideas on a topic is with computer freewriting. With computer freewriting, you write without rules or restraints. Computer freewriting is unguided writing – writing done quickly and without any planning.

Step 1. Open a document and **Save** it as "Computer Freewriting."

Step 2. After making certain your cursor is at the far left position, turn off your computer monitor. When your screen is dark and you are directed to type, begin typing as fast and as furiously as you can – whatever ideas pop into your head. You can begin writing without having any particular topic in mind at all. What is important is that once you begin typing, you do not stop for at least four minutes. If you find yourself writing nonsense, that's okay. Just don't stop. Don't worry about correct punctuation, spelling, or grammar rules.

Step 3. When you are directed to stop at the end of four minutes, turn on your monitors and look over what you have written.

Step 4. With your cursor, **Highlight** and then **Bold** those ideas you have repeated or that seem more interesting or appealing to you than others.

Step 5. Select one of the topics you have bolded and think about it for a few minutes. Then turn your monitor off again and freewrite again for at least five minutes.

Step 6. Turn on your monitor and look at what you have written. Again, **Bold** those ideas that seem more interesting or appealing to you than others. **Save** your work. From what you have written, come up with at least one idea for a topic for a paper.

Word Pictures

Nature scenes, works of art, and photographs often stimulate writers' imaginations. This quiet group activity asks students to write about an inspiring picture, then add on to another person's work. The more sophisticated or complex the pictures are, the more demanding the task often becomes.

Once you have completed this in-class activity, it can be repeated with students writing about pictures they have found on their own.

Special Notes:

- This activity requires students to move quietly from computer to computer to collaborate on each other's writing.
- You will need to provide the class with at least one picture to write about. This picture can be a photograph, a painting or another work of art. For variety, you can have students write about different pictures. In this case, place a different picture at each computer work station.

Word Pictures

Scenes in nature, works of art, and photographs often stimulate writers' imaginations. With this exercise, you will use a picture your teacher has given to you as inspiration for writing.

Step 1. Study the picture your teacher has asked you to use for writing inspiration. What does it suggest to you? What does it make you feel? What details describe it? Does it give you an idea for a story? What characters will you use to relate the idea of the picture? How many characters will you need? What details of the setting will you emphasize? What will be the theme or significance of the event or situation you are describing?

Step 2. Open a new document in your word processing program and Save it as "Word Picture." Put your name, class, and date in the top right-hand corner.

Step 3. Begin freewriting, reacting in some way to the picture. You might simply describe the picture. You might choose to treat the picture as an illustration of an event in a story, an incident in an actual person's life, or as a still frame from a movie. You might write a short story, a newspaper report, or even a letter. Be creative. Use metaphors and similes as you write, as well as vivid and precise details.

Step 4. Write until you are told to stop. Type the word "STOP" in bold, capital letters at the end of your writing. Save what you have written, and then move to another computer.

Step 5. On the new computer screen, read what your classmate has written and then continue his/her description or narrative. In other words, put yourself in the other writer's shoes and continue what he or she has started. As you write, continue to use vivid metaphors and similes, as well as vivid and precise details.

Step 6. Continue writing until you are told to stop. Again, type the word "STOP" in bold, capital letters. Save what you have written, and then move to another computer.

Step 7. Continue, repeating steps five and six, above, until the end of the class hour. Save your work. Then Print copies equal to the number of individuals who worked at the computer where you are currently working, plus one for the teacher.

Step 8. Keep a copy, give your instructor a copy, and place the remaining copies at the computer for others to collect. Be sure to collect copies of the responses at each computer where you worked.

creative writing

Sniglets

"Sniglets" are words that *ought* to be in the dictionary, but aren't. They are words coined to describe or define a situation when no existing word does the job. Most sniglets are created by stringing together words or appropriate parts of words, usually in an imaginative or humorous way.

Comedian Rich Hall introduced the concept of sniglets on *Saturday Night Live* shows in 1984. Since then, he has published a series of entertaining books on the subject.

The exercise of creating sniglets round-robin style is one way to stir students' creative juices. It is also an excellent introduction to the study of language, as it demonstrates a common practice of ancient and Elizabethan playwrights. Shakespeare introduced new words into the vocabulary each time he wrote plays, sometimes creating them by combining whole words or parts of words. Here are some examples:

- BREED-BATE: a breeder of debate, a fomenter of quarrels
- CANDLE-WASTERS: persons who sit up all night to drink
- LASS-LORN: deserted by a mistress

The exercise that follows encourages students to turn their imaginations loose to create new words. So as to provide them some direction, they are asked to create words that fit particular categories. You can use the ones listed below, or add your own.

Special Notes:

- Before class begins, assign one of the following categories to each computer in your lab: *food, education, politics, finances, entertainment, people, animals, sports* and *work*. Using a self-stick note or piece of paper, label each computer with its category name.

- Students will need to move from computer to computer for this collaborative activity. You can direct this by allowing students a set amount of time at each computer, or you can allow students to move to any other open computer whenever they are finished with one category.

Sniglets

Comedian Rich Hall introduced the concept of sniglets on a series of *Saturday Night Live* shows in 1984. According to Hall, sniglets are "words that *ought* to be in the dictionary, but aren't." They are usually created by putting together existing words, or parts of existing words.

Here are a few examples of sniglets created by students. Can you identify the root words or parts of words from which they are created?

SAMPLE SNIGLETS

paraislesis: the phenomenon that occurs when whatever aisle or line you have chosen at the grocery store or ticket counter immediately stops moving

cashabyss: small space between your outstretched fingers and the ATM so that you have to unbuckle your safety belt and open your car door to reach it

dentaremorse: that nasty feeling in your mouth that reminds you when you are traveling that you forgot your toothbrush

aromostale: the stale, sweaty stench found in wrestling rooms

sleazify: what the press inevitably does to any person who becomes well-known

---

Try your hand at creating some sniglets. In brainstorming ideas for your new words, open your mind. Play with ideas. Think how everyday life relates to the categories listed below.

Step 1. Each computer is labeled with one of the following categories:

- food
- education
- politics
- finances
- entertainment
- people
- animals
- sports
- work

Choose a computer with a category you want to try first. Then Open a new document in your word processing program and Save it as "Sniglets." If you are the first person at your computer station, type the name of the category at the top of the document.

Step 2. Create at least one sniglet for the category listed on your computer. Remember that a sniglet is simply a made-up word, usually created by combining two real words. For example, a sniglet for the category "Food" might be "*musquirt*: the little squirt of water that comes out of a mustard bottle if you don't shake it well." The word is created by combining part of the word "mustard" and "squirt."

Step 3. Put your initials after each entry you write. Here's how the first entry on a computer might look:

SAMPLE SNIGLET ENTRY

FOOD

fridgeatrophy: the shriveling process that affects products forgotten in the bottom of the refrigerator (J.C.)

Step 4. When you have finished creating at least one sniglet, Save your work, move to another computer, and create a sniglet on a new topic. (Remember to put your initials in parentheses after each entry you write.)

Step 5. At the end of class, Save the file at the computer where you are sitting. Print two copies of the sniglet document. Keep one and turn in the other to be placed in a binder to share with the class.

Collaboration Stories

With "Collaboration Stories," students work together while also working independently, thus allowing one student's ideas to stimulate another's imagination. The story lines will take some very imaginative twists and turns, demonstrating the old concept that two heads are better than one.

Allow three class periods for the project. In the first lab, students will set up their stories and begin writing them. Every 10-15 minutes, they will switch computers and continue writing a different story. This process will be continued in the second lab, with each student eventually finishing a story and then editing it.

In the third lab, students will share their stories. You may want to allow them to read aloud in small groups, or you may want to have them pass the stories around to share silently.

In addition to aiding students, the teacher's role is that of timekeeper, telling students when it is time to switch computers. (Depending upon the length of your classes and the age of your students, each writing session should last 10-15 minutes.) As this is an ambitious project, you will have to watch the time closely.

Collaboration Stories

Sometimes, just for fun, groups write a novel in round-robin fashion, passing it from one person to the next to add to the story. With this activity, you and your classmates will collaborate to write several short stories during the next two lab periods.

Many of you are probably familiar with the TV show "Whose Line Is It Anyway?" In this show, the host provides the actors with brief prompts, which they develop on the spot, often creating side-splitting comedy. In this spirit, you and your classmates will give some brief prompts for others to use in creating a story.

Computer Lab #1:

Step 1. Start by planning the basic features of a short story. First, decide what kind of story you want to write: mystery, suspense, action, romance, etc. Who will be the audience for this kind of story?

Step 2. Open a new document in your word processing program and Save it as "Story Started by (Your Name)." Then create a table similar to the one below.

Principal Features of the Story			
Characteristics of two main characters 1. 2.	Time Period	Setting	Major Conflicts

(In Microsoft Word, click on **Table**, *then* **Insert**, *then* **Table**. *Then choose "4" for the number of columns and "3" for the number of rows. It is easiest to select* **Fixed Column Width** *under the* **AutoFit Behavior** *section. In earlier versions of Word, click on* **Table**, *then* **Insert Table**. *Fill in "4" for the number of columns and "3" for the number of rows.*

If you are using a different program, consult your **Help** *menu to see how you create a table. Look for the word "table" in the* **Help Index**.)

Step 3. Once you have created the table, Save it. Now create two main characters for your story. In the first column of the table, list the name of each character and five or six physical and personality characteristics.

Step 4. Choose one of the remaining three features in the table: "Time Period," "Setting," or "Major Conflicts." Fill in details about this *one* feature. For example, if you choose "Major Conflicts," you will need to think about what conflicts might be involved. Will the characters struggle with each other? For what reason? Will they join forces to oppose some outside agent? Who or what will it be? Will they struggle against nature? Why and for what reason?

When you are finished, you should have filled in the table for only two of the four principal features of the story. **Save** these additions.

Step 5. Now switch computers with one of your classmates. At the second computer, complete the table that has been started. You decide on the details of the two remaining features in the table. For example, if the first person filled in "Character" and "Time Period," you fill in the details for "Setting" and "Major Conflicts." When you are finished, **Save** your work. Here is an example of a completed table:

Sample Completed Table			
Characteristics of two main characters	Time Period	Setting	Major Conflicts
1. Charlene. A waitress at the Buffalope Truck Stop. She is 55 and skinny. She calls everyone "hon." She mothers everyone. She gets great tips because everyone loves her. 2. Beaumont Jacoby. A wealthy investor. He is 45, wears a custom-made three piece suit, and small, tasteful glasses. His taste runs to opera, fine art, and travel. He wears a toupee.	The story takes place in the present.	The story takes place at the Buffalope Truck Stop in rural Wyoming, where Beaumont's limousine has run into mechanical problems.	The major conflict will be between Beaumont and Charlene. She will refuse to treat him any differently than any of the truckers or tourists who stop in. He will struggle to remain aloof and resist her efforts to treat him like one of the guys. There will also be a struggle between the chauffeur and Claude, the owner of the only repair shop for miles.

Step 6. Switch computers again with a classmate. Do not return to the computer where you began. (In fact, each time you switch during this activity, you should always be at a different computer station.) Study the characteristics filled in under "Principal Features of the Story."

Step 7. Write an opening couple of paragraphs for a story, using the features listed on the table. As you write, remember to **Save** frequently. Write until your teacher says, "Switch."

Step 8. From this point on, whenever your teacher says, "Switch," stop writing and move on to another computer. Each time you move, review the information on the table and read the part of the story that has already been written. Beginning where the previous writer left off, continue the story. *(Note: You will have approximately 15 minutes to write each time you move. The stories will not be finished in this lab period.)*

Step 9. When you are given the two-minute signal that the first lab is about to end, Save to disk all that has been written, under the title already given to the file by the person opening the file.

Step 10. Close the word processing program. Label the disk with the name of the file, and turn it in.

Computer Lab #2

During this lab, you will continue the stories begun in the previous lab and write an ending for one of them.

Step 1. Pick up a disk – not the one you turned in after the last lab. Open the file containing the short story that was begun in the previous lab.

Step 2. Read all that was written last lab period, and then begin developing the story from the point where the writer left off.

Step 3. Again, when you are told to switch, save what you have written to disk, and move to a new story. (Note: You will have two 10 to 15-minute sessions to work on the draft of a story, each at a different computer.)

Step 4. After two switches, you will be at a computer station with a story for which you are to write an ending and revise as much as you can in the time remaining. Use your Spelling and Grammar check to make superficial changes. Complex changes will have to be done by rearranging sentences, even chapters, and substituting and adding words/phrases. Do your best in the time allowed.

Step 5. At the end of the class period, Save to disk what you have completed, even if you are not finished, and Print two copies, one for yourself and one to turn in.

Step 6. During the next class period, you will be called upon to share your final story, either by reading it aloud in a group or by passing it to others for silent reading. Read through your story before the next class, and remember to bring your copy to share.

Musical Composition

Music is an important element in most students' lives, but few have used it as a basis for writing. "Musical Composition" allows them to use music to stimulate their imaginations as they write.

As most young people prefer contemporary music, it often proves interesting to introduce them to a classical composition and let that piece of music be the stimulus for their writing. Many classical works can be effective. Here are just a few suggestions:

- Beethoven's *Symphony No. 5*
- Liszt's *Hungarian Rhapsody*
- Offenbach's *Orphée aux enfers* (Orpheus in the Underworld)
- Haydn's *Symphony No. 94*
- Brahms' *Festival Overture*
- Mozart's *Serenade No. 13* (Eine kleine Nachtmusik)
- Tchaikovsky's *1812 Festival Overture*

Before you select a work to use with a class, listen to it yourself and decide which ten-minute segment of the composition will likely prove most stimulating for your group of students.

After you play the excerpt you have selected for the class, you may want to play it a second time. Because an exciting idea sometimes comes to a student toward the end of listening to a piece, he or she may need time to listen again and add additional details.

"Musical Composition" is broken into three stages. The exercise as a whole requires at least two lab periods, as it is unlikely that students will be able to complete their compositions in 25 minutes.

In addition to selecting the music and supervising the activity, you are also the time-keeper. The student directions describe your time-keeping responsibilities.

(This exercise was developed from a class exercise originated by Jennifer Arameish, a West Liberty State College English Education major.)

Musical Composition

Almost everyone enjoys music, and for a variety of reasons. It entertains. It relaxes. It often inspires. With "Musical Composition," you will let a classical composition be your inspiration for writing. Although you may be more accustomed to other types of music, you will find classical music can be a great stimulus for writing.

Stage #1:

Step 1. During the lab period, you will be listening to a classical composition for approximately 10 minutes. (After you have finished the exercise, the composer, artist, and name of the piece will be revealed.) To prepare for your listening and composing experience, Open a new document and Save it to your disk under the title "Musical Composition." Once you have done this, you are ready to begin.

Step 2. While you are listening to the music, record in your new document the many thoughts, emotions, and images that come into your mind as you listen. Don't try to organize what flows through your mind. Simply record it. Do not try to tell a story. Just write down whatever comes to mind as you listen. If you need to close your eyes from time to time to really see the images in your mind, do so. Allow yourself to "be" in the music.

Step 3. When you are told to stop, Save what you have written. (If you need more time to develop the ideas the music suggested to you, ask your teacher to play the excerpt again.)

Step 4. When you are finished, Print one copy of your draft composition.

Stage #2:

Step 1. Exchange the printed copy of your "Musical Composition" thoughts with a classmate. Read through the classmate's paper carefully.

Step 2. Use your classmate's ideas as the basis for a short story. Open a new document and Save it under an appropriate title. Then start writing, letting the ideas you find on your classmate's page dictate whether you write a fantasy, a romance, a children's story, an adventure, or a science fiction story. You will have approximately 25 minutes to develop a plot. Remember: Use the words and phrases you find in your classmate's paper as the basis for your story.

Step 3. When you are told to stop writing, Save what you have written to disk, even if you are not completely finished. Print one copy.

Stage #3:

Step 1. Form a group of four with other members of your class. Within your group, have each group member read aloud the story he or she has written. Discuss the strengths and weaknesses of the story and make suggestions for improvement.

Step 2. When everyone is finished reading, identify the most successful story in your group. Determine who will read it to the class. (It doesn't need to be the person who wrote the story.)

Step 3. After each group has chosen its best story, listen as someone from each group reads aloud the story the group selected. As a class, discuss the story's strengths and weaknesses, focusing on setting, plot, and character development. Examine what methods or details create interest and understanding and also what information or details are still needed to increase understanding and entertain the reader.

Step 4. After you have heard all the stories, you should have more ideas for ways to improve your own story. Return to your computer to revise and polish your story.

Step 5. Be certain you have titled your story and identified both yourself and the author of the original ideas in the top right-hand corner of the first page. Finish the revision, Save it to disk, and Print two copies. Turn in one.

Step 6. Bring a copy of your story to the next class. Your teacher will ask that you share your story in one of two ways: by passing it around for others to read to themselves, or by reading it aloud to the class.

creative writing

Myth Brochure

"Myth Brochure" makes an excellent culminating exercise for a unit on mythology. With this activity, students create a brochure to attract visitors to their town or city. However, they exaggerate and embellish real features to create mythological elements. They use their imaginations to characterize the unusual features of their communities and neighborhoods as though they were parts of a myth.

Students can create their brochures with any word processing program. However, a program like Microsoft Publisher makes the creation of a brochure especially easy. Students can use the step-by-step "wizard" feature to lead them through the process.

The activity requires two or more lab periods for actual work on the brochure. An alternative is to set up the exercise in a supervised lab and then allow students to complete the brochure as homework. In either case, students will have to do some field research; that is, they will have to take notes about their community or neighborhood so that they have solid information to work from when they begin the lab exercise.

Myth Brochure

With "Myth Brochure," you will create a brochure that invites travelers to experience some of the wonder and mystery of your own town or city. However, your brochure will treat your town or city as though it were part of a mythological story. You will exaggerate, twist and embellish real features to create a work of fiction. You will call attention to the town's mythical figures and its glorious (or difficult!) origin. You will create your own gods and goddesses, heroes and heroines and call attention to your "kingdom's" origin. You will definitely need to use your imagination!

Before you begin, take a look at the sample brochures on pages 84-87. They may give you ideas for the kinds of things you might include in your brochure.

Homework

Step 1. Mythology and folklore are a part of every ancient and modern civilization. With mythology, people try to explain the mysteries of their origin as a nation and the unpredictable elements of their nation's geography.

To familiarize yourself somewhat with myths from other cultures, log on to a web site and read at least two myths – not folklore – from another country. D. L. Ashliman, a retired University of Pittsburgh Professor, has compiled one of the most complete listings of these stories of past and present civilizations at this web site:

http://www.pitt.edu/~dash/ashliman.html

You might also consult *Mythweb*, a web site devoted to the heroes, gods and monsters of Greek mythology:

http://www.mythweb.com/

Step 2. Next do some field research about the community you live in. You may even want to focus on just your neighborhood.

What you are looking for with your field research is subject matter that has the potential for exaggeration. All of us have unusual neighbors, houses, pets, etc., that can be fodder for myth and fantasy. Look for features that will help you present your community as an exciting, fascinating place that people would want to explore.

For example, the author of this book has a Jack Russell Terrier that is a legend on his block. The young men at the nearby Sigma Nu fraternity house fear him because he manages, at least once a week, to interrupt their volleyball game by stealing the ball. He's earned the nickname Kujo Jack, after Stephen King's monster dog. A myth brochure about this neighborhood might easily exaggerate this dog's accomplishments.

To collect the information you need, play the reporter, recording numerous details. Organize your information into these categories:

- Descriptive details about two "gods" or "goddesses" that populate your mythical kingdom. Look for at least two people, or even pets or animals, that you can develop into exciting heroic or villainous figures.

- Descriptive details about the geography of your neighborhood — the weather, the seasons, the animals, the unique qualities of its landscape.

- Descriptive details about two particular attractions or activities of the area — historical landmarks, unusual buildings or houses, annual events, etc.

- Other categories appropriate to your specific community or neighborhood.

Step 3. Collect pictures or drawings suitable to include in your brochure. You may already have some pictures you've taken of neighborhood or community events and/or people. These can be scanned and used in your layout. Of course, digital photos are a possibility as well.

You might also download free photographs or clip art from the Internet. You can easily find sites by doing a search for "free clip art" or "free photographs." Be sure to read the End User License Agreement (EULA) at any site you use. Sometimes there are certain restrictions on the use of an item. For example, the EULA may forbid posting the picture on a web site, or it may prohibit resale of the item. Most often, for personal or educational use, there are few restrictions, if any.

When you finish the homework steps, above, proceed to instructions below.

Creating your brochure

Step 1. Create a new document and Save it as "Myth Brochure." If you are using a program with a "wizard," like Microsoft Publisher, read through all of the following steps to familiarize yourself with the requirements of the brochure. Then allow the wizard to lead you through the steps in creating a three-fold brochure.

If you are using a word processing program, set up a Landscape oriented document with margins of .5 on all four sides.

(In Microsoft Word, click File, *then* Page Setup. *Select .5 for each margin. Then choose the* Paper Size *tab and select* Landscape. *Click* OK.*)*.

Step 2. There are many ways to create a brochure. You may choose any design or layout method you like. One easy method is to set up your document so that it is two pages long, with three columns to a page.

(In Microsoft Word, select Format, *then* Column, *then* Three. *If you like, hit* Enter *over and over again, so that you can see the three columns. To go to the top of the next column, hit* Ctrl Shift Enter. *If you are on the third column and would like to create a second page, hit* Ctrl Shift Enter, *and a second page will appear.)*

Your document will consist of two pages. However, when it is printed front to back, it will consist of only one page. Here's how the two pages will be laid out:

EXAMPLE

inside flap	back of brochure	front of brochure

inside left of brochure	inside center of brochure	inside right of brochure

Step 3. Now you are ready to start designing your brochure. What items will you include? Where will you put each picture? What will go on the front? What will go on the back? What headlines will you include? What text will you need to write?

Sketch out a plan for your brochure on paper before you begin.

Step 4. Start by adding headlines where you need them in a font larger than your basic text font. Then insert pictures and clip art wherever you want them. Remember to **Save** frequently.

Step 5. Now begin writing the copy for your brochure. You may type it directly into the brochure, or you may start a new file and type it there, copying it into your brochure when you are finished.

Step 6. After your copy is all in place, begin editing the brochure. You may need to re-size pictures and headings in order to make everything fit in an attractive way. You may also want to add color, borders, shading, etc. Don't expect everything to work out perfectly the first time!

(In Microsoft Word, see **Format** *for many options, including borders, bullets and number-ing, and background colors. See* **Insert** *for information about using* **WordArt***, inserting* **Clip Art***,* **Photographs***, and more.)*

Step 7. When you think you have a brochure that works, **Print** a "tester" and try folding the brochure as follows:

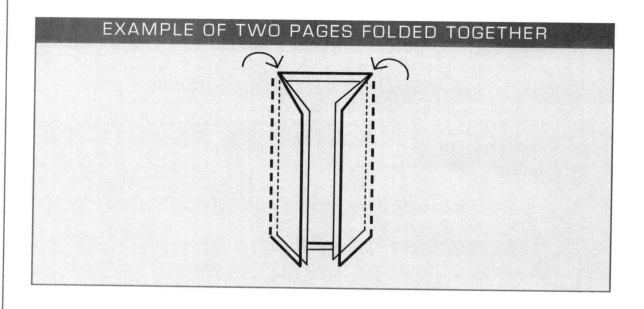

EXAMPLE OF TWO PAGES FOLDED TOGETHER

Step 8. Check your test brochure carefully. Do things line up the way you want them to? Does anything need to be moved or changed? Make any adjustments that are necessary.

Step 9. Save and Print your final copy. Because you will want your final brochure to be printed on just one piece of paper, you will need to run the paper through the printer twice. First, you will need to figure out which side of paper your printer prints on. (It varies from printer to printer). Print one test copy. Then Print three copies of the front side. Turn them over and re-feed them into the printer to print the second side.

Step 10. Fold your brochures. Keep one, and turn one in. The other copy is to share with the class.

mythology and writing

Experience the Wonders of Bethania

Home of Bison the Great

Don't miss the Bethania Bison Birthday Festival!

When you visit Bethania, don't miss Riverside Park, a center for family gatherings and celebrations in the summer. It's also the site of the annual Bethania Bison Birthday Festival, which pays tribute to founder Bison the Great.

The Most Challenging Whitewater in the World

Encircling the village of Bethania is one of the most challenging whitewater streams in the world – The Buffalo. The Buffalo received its name from the numerous herds of bison roaming the area in days gone by. The legendary Bison the Great was able to tame and domesticate the numerous herds of bison, but he was never able to tame the wild waters of the Buffalo.

The world's greatest athletes and fishermen are drawn to the Buffalo in all seasons, accepting its challenge of swift currents, rocky narrows, and turbulent waters. However, few have captured any of the three-foot rainbow trout and catfish that thrive in its swift currents, for even in winter, the Frost Gods are unable to slow its waters.

mythology and writing

SAMPLE MYTH BROCHURE #1 (SIDE TWO)

Bethania – a village rich in history

Because of the mountainous, densely forested terrain, the first settlers in what is now Bethania faced a gargantuan task in their attempt to tame the wilderness. Try as they might, most of them were able to clear only a small patch of land to grow enough food to make it through the harsh winters.

That all changed when Bison, a hardy young man found roaming with a herd of buffalo, was befriended by a hermit. (See left.) When the herd moved on, Bison stayed. It was not long before he took it upon himself to clear land along the turbulent river that encircled the rich bottom land. It was in this loamy, dark soil that the village of Bethania would take root and grow.

A tribute to the hermit. After the hermit's death, Bison felt compelled to share what he had learned. He invited the children of settlers into a crude but inviting lodge he had built from the virgin forests. There he taught the children what he had learned under the wise old hermit.

As the years passed, the farm Bison developed flourished, and he used the money he earned from it to establish a school for the children of the settlers. Later he founded a church called the "Meeting House," based on the simple belief that all humans are loved by God. The log Meeting House was replaced well over a century ago by a glorious brick structure, which remains today in the center of Bethania.

Who Was Bison the Great?

Bison the Great was named after the creatures he roamed with as a child. In 1820, when he was twenty years of age, he was taken in by a hermit who lived in the foothills near present-day Bethania. Legend has it that Bison came upon the hermit as he sat reading a Greek classic. Hearing the strange words the hermit read aloud, Bison grew curious. Gesturing and grunting, even sometimes pawing the ground, he made it known that he wanted to learn to read. Under the gentle, encouraging tutelage of this hermit, Bison became a voracious reader of the classics.

Settlers in the untamed northern panhandle of what later would be called West Virginia delighted in telling stories about Bison. They claimed that, after working most of the day clearing trees to create pasture for the buffalo he

had tamed or digging tunnels through mountains, he would sit by the light of the hermit's fire reading Cicero, Plato, and Socrates. The settlers swore they often heard him read lengthy passages in Greek to the hermit, and then translate what he had read into English.

Bison's spirit lives on. It was these early studies that inspired Bison the Great to develop the village of Bethania, a cultural center in the foothills of northern West Virginia. Many claim they feel Bison's presence when they walk the shores of the Buffalo River. Some have reported hearing his voice echoing in the foothills. Still others swear that they feel his eyes on them as they visit such local establishments as the Chambers Family Grocery.

Chambers Family Grocery
A popular Bethania institution where Bison the Great's spirit is said to lurk

The Bison Bridge
The longest green bridge in the world

SAMPLE MYTH BROCHURE #2 (SIDE ONE)

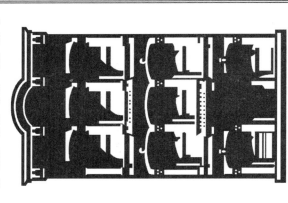

The HARPER

Not an ordinary apartment building

BALTIMORE, MARYLAND

THE LAUNDRY ROOM. The Laundry Room, situated in the underbelly of The Harper, is the home to many devilish imps. These Laundry Room imps have fun by taking wet clothes out of a washing machine and putting them in a sopping pile on top of the machine. They are also known to put something red in a load of whites and steal random socks.

Since The Laundry Room houses the only door to The Dumpster, it often becomes a makeshift dumping ground for people's unwanted garbage. The rotting trash combined with the mildew of soaking wet clothes can create a putrid odor that infiltrates the entire building. The faint of heart need not even approach The Laundry Room.

THE FIRE CHUTE. The Harper, a many-storied apartment building, has no fire escape. Instead, it has The Fire Chute. The Fire Chute is basically a 14-story slide in the center of the building. No one can remember the last time The Fire Chute was used for an actual fire. However, sometimes something can be heard thunking down it in the middle of the night. Legend has it that the Fire Chute Monster grabs unsuspecting visitors and tosses them down the chute whenever he is bored.

SEE THE SCARY SIDE

OF

The Harper

The Greeks had Hades. Dante wrote about The Inferno. The Harper has equally scary places. For those who love danger, these areas can really get the adrenaline pumping!

THE DUMPSTER. The Dumpster is truly a dangerous place at The Harper. After the sun sets, you can be a victim to numerous untold crimes if you are out at The Dumpster. This means that residents of The Harper are forced to take out all smelly trash only during daylight hours. It is commonly believed that it is much better to live with rank garbage than to risk a night trip to The Dumpster, where various dangerous Dumpster devils lurk.

SAMPLE MYTH BROCHURE #2 (SIDE TWO)

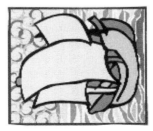

The Harper is an apartment building in Baltimore, Maryland.

Named after an early leader in colonial America, the building has a long and rich history.

Located in the midst of majestic churches and yummy ethnic restaurants, *The Harper* is a neighborhood full of mythical creatures.

The Harper is a magical world full of unusual creatures. Here are just a few of the interesting characters that lurk throughout and around the apartment building:

CRAZY BLONDE GUY. Every neighborhood needs at least one local eccentric, and Harper Street, the street next to The Harper, has Crazy Blonde Guy. Not usually scary, he can be seen walking in a zig-zag fashion, spitting and muttering to himself. According to local legend, Crazy Blonde Guy was also once seen walking the streets wearing nothing but an umbrella.

THE STOMPINGTONS. An annoying bunch of creatures lives on the 13th floor of The Harper. They are commonly referred to as The Stompingtons. The most obvious characteristic of The Stompingtons is their incessant stomping, which usually occurs after the sun goes down. Every step they take makes a thunderous roar to the neighbors living beneath them. They also commit other noisy shenanigans while others try to sleep, such as playing PlayStation at top volume and having rowdy weeknight parties.

THE SMELLIVANS. The Smellivans are mischievous gremlins who pipe interesting smells throughout The Harper. Sometimes, if you are lucky, The Smellivans will create wonderful, delicious smells, such as warm chocolate brownies, tangy curry or jasmine incense. When you are not so lucky, they create the stinking stench of reeking cabbage, burnt microwave popcorn or an overflowing diaper genie.

Family Newspaper

A publication that usually includes a variety of writing styles is the local newspaper. Having students create a family newspaper of their own is an excellent way for them to review and practice many kinds of writing.

Students can work alone on this project or in teams. As it is an ambitious project, it can work well as an end-of-the semester independent project.

writing and designing

Family Newspaper

Don't have time to talk to family members? Too burdened by homework, a part-time job and extra-curricular activities to socialize with your kid brother? With "Family Newspaper," you will have a chance to communicate with your family and complete a major school assignment at the same time. You will be creating a family newspaper based on *your* family. (You can write about your biological family, your adoptive family, your school family, your church family — whatever family you choose.)

The process of creating the newspaper is divided into three parts:

Part 1:   Planning
Part 2:   Creating a layout format for each page
Part 3:   Writing text for each page to fit the space you have allowed for the articles and ads

Part I

Step 1. The first step in creating a family newspaper is planning. What will your family newspaper include? Take a look at your local paper to stimulate your imagination. As you look through it, jot down ideas for your own newspaper. At the very least, your newspaper should include the following:

- A front page containing one major story and two or three minor ones on noteworthy family achievements or events. (Ideas: upcoming competitions, anniversaries, birthdays, job changes, awards, vacations, etc.) These accounts can be serious, straightforward, humorous, even fictitious. Don't overlook the possibility of articles related to past achievements or past events. For example, you might have an article on the tenth anniversary of moving into the family home, or the first anniversary of adopting your dog from the local pound.

- At least one editorial. Topics might include subjects such as "Our Current Curfew is Unfair," "New Rules Needed for Borrowing the Family Car," or "Taco Tuesday Should Be Replaced."

- Two feature stories. These might be on any topic of interest to the family, such as pet care, budgeting, nutrition, or car maintenance, for example.

- Entertainment section. This section might include an advice column, television or movie reviews, a horoscope, a crossword puzzle, cartoons, a gossip column, fashion pointers, or other items.

- Advertisements. Include advertisements throughout your newspaper. You might include ads for items popular with your family, classified ads, personal ads (seeking a companion for a family member or pet, for example), ads for movies or events, ads for stores or businesses, or other ads.

- A sports and activities page containing accounts of past, present, and future sporting events.

writing and designing

Step 2. Decide whether your newspaper will take a serious approach or a humorous approach to your family news. You might also choose a blend of humorous and straightforward reporting.

Step 3. Do some mental role-playing. Pretend you are someone else – your father, mother, sister, brother, or grandparent, for example. If that person were to make a contribution to your newspaper, what would it be? A guest editorial? An advice column? A sports article? A political cartoon? An advertisement? Or . . . ? Jot down your ideas.

Step 4. Gather some appropriate photographs to go with the stories. You can scan family photographs or use digital photographs. Another possibility is downloading generic photographs from a free-use web site. (Try doing a search for "free photographs." Be sure to read the license agreement carefully.)

Part II

Now that you have determined the type and number of articles on each page, you need to create a layout. (If you are using a design program such as Microsoft Publisher, just follow the steps of the newsletter "Wizard" and skip ahead to Part III.)

If you are using a word processing program, the process will be a bit harder. There are several ways to go about creating a layout, but the method described below is fairly easy and allows for adjustments later.

Step 1. Start by sketching out a design for the front page of your newspaper on a piece of paper. On the next page is an example of a front page layout design. Of course, you can vary this design to suit your own needs.

Step 2. Open a new document and **Save** it as "Family Newspaper." Set your margins for .5 or .6, on all four sides.

*(In Microsoft Word, go to **File** and choose **Page Setup**, then **Margins**. Set top, bottom, left, and right margins for .5 or .6.)*

Step 3. Now start inserting text boxes for your design.

*(In Microsoft Word, click on **Insert**, then **Text Box**. Place your cursor where you want to locate the box, and click on your mouse. A text box will appear. Drag the mouse to create the size box you want. To move or reposition the box, click on it. Move your mouse over it until a cross appears. Then click your mouse and drag the box into position.)*

Part III

Step 1. Now you are ready to start creating the text for your stories. Using the notes you brainstormed, start writing. You can write directly into your newspaper layout, or you

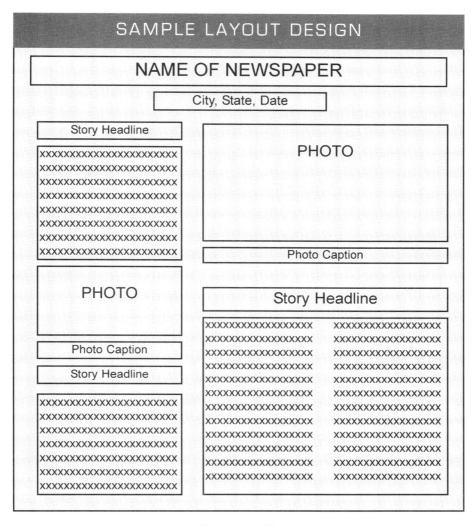

SAMPLE LAYOUT DESIGN

NAME OF NEWSPAPER

City, State, Date

Story Headline

PHOTO

Photo Caption

PHOTO

Story Headline

Photo Caption

Story Headline

can write in another document and then Copy and Paste your work into the newspaper layout as you finish it. As you write, remember that reporters always answer the five Ws: Who? What? Where? When? Why? and also How?

Step 2. Of course, you will also need to type in headlines. When you write your headlines, use present tense and active verbs, and delete the articles "a," "an," and "the." You may also want to eliminate all but the most essential words. (Example: Instead of writing, "John and Mary Herbert celebrate their fiftieth wedding anniversary," write, "Herberts celebrate fiftieth.")

Step 3. Next add your photographs.

To add photographs in Microsoft Word, click on Insert, then Picture, then From File. Select the location of your saved photograph.

Be sure to write captions for each photograph. Captions generally include a verb, rather than just a label. Here are some examples:

> ### SAMPLE CAPTIONS
>
> *Pictured above: Members of the soccer team.*
> *Proud Grandpa Lopez shows off new granddaughter.*
> *Kevin examines hail damage to new car.*

Step 4. Remember to Save regularly. Once you have finished the first page, you are ready to develop the remaining pages. The process is the same for each page as it was for the front page. The only additional item you will need is a "page tag" at the upper left or right corner of each page. Put it on the left if the page is on the left of a two-page layout as you open the paper. Put it on the right if it is on the right of the two-page layout. See below for an example:

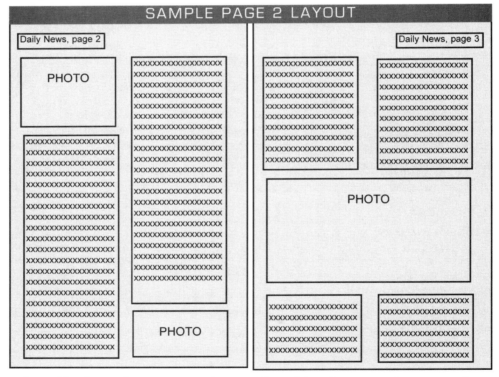

SAMPLE PAGE 2 LAYOUT

You can also add other information to the tag, if you like. For example, you might include the hometown and state, date, or the volume and issue number.

Step 5. After you have completed your four-page newspaper, proofread carefully. Save your work. Then Print out three copies: one to turn in, one for yourself, and one to share with the class. All printers differ, so you may need to experiment to have your newspaper print correctly.

Cole Family's
No.1 Choice

The Cole Herald Star

Bethany, West Virginia

Volume 1, Issue 1 — April 1, 2003

Cole re-elected Mt. de Chantal class president

Mt. de Chantal student Devon Cole was elected by acclamation president of her junior class. This is her seventh year as class president, having served as president of various classes since the fifth grade.

Using the campaign slogan "Leadership for a New Century," Cole outlined an ambitious array of activities for the junior class, designed to involve all class members.

The activities included a volunteer after-school tutorial program for middle school children in the Wheeling area, a Support Your Troops letter campaign, and the establishment of honoraries in a variety of disciplines.

The John Cole family dog Russell, pictured above, was selected for a West Liberty State College television commercial.

J.G. Cole's dorm room, pictured above, was declared the cleanest on WVU's Main Campus

Cole dorm room selected

West Virginia University Vice President of Campus Life Dale Evans announced that John Griffin Cole's Tyler Residence Hall room will be photographed for inclusion in a campus life booklet for Admissions. The room was cited as an outstanding example of cleanliness.

Cole, a sophomore majoring in biochemistry, was pleased with the selection of his room. "My mother will go into shock when she hears about this," Cole said. "My father used to make weekly raids with garbage bags to make a path through my room." Cole looks forward to future employment with Merry Maids.

Beloved Cole family pet dog chosen for West Liberty State College commercial

by Robyn Cole

Russell, the beloved family pet of the John Cole family for the past 11 years, will be featured in a TV commercial created by West Liberty State College Sigma Tau Delta members.

The English Honorary designed a college comforter to earn money for the society's academic activities. In looking for a unique way to advertise it, the students discovered Russell's love for the comforter.

"Russell's first choice of a place to nap is the comforter on the family room sofa," explained John Cole, an English professor at the college and advisor to Sigma Tau Delta.

The commercial is to be developed by TV majors in the communications department. It will be a 60-second spot airing on the campus network and West Liberty's local cable system.

"Russell is a real pro," commented Diane Williams, the TV major in charge of designing and overseeing the production of the commercial. "He's really incredible. It took only one walk-through for him to learn what he was supposed to do," Williams said.

Sigma Tau Delta members hope this unusual sales approach will be just the right one to bring in the orders. The first airing of the commercial is scheduled for the week of April 7.

Cole's chili wins award

In a West Liberty State College Campus Ministry Chili Cook-off, English professor John Cole's vegetarian chili was voted the People's Choice.

Students, faculty, and staff declared it the best of ten entries in the annual cook-off. Cole said he developed the recipe when three of his children became vegetarian.

An April Fools' Day edition of the author's family newspaper

SAMPLE FAMILY NEWSPAPER #1 (PAGE 2)

Cole Herald Star   Page 2

Cole family study reports child rearing increases parental anxiety levels

In a recent study for a behavior and social science class project, Brooke High School sophomore Seth Cole interviewed the parents of over 200 Brooke High School students. His study focused on questions designed to see if certain age levels cause parental anxiety to increase.

Parents of students in grades 9-12 were selected at random for the study. Cole was also careful to make certain that the study involved mixed genders and family sizes.

Overwhelmingly, the results of the study reinforced the widely held belief that teenage years are the most difficult for parents. One mother commented, "Life in our family was blissful until our two children entered puberty." Another parent claimed, "The dinner table was sometimes a battle zone. Arguments became so intense my wife and I considered using only plastic utensils."

Cole will present his project at the school science fair April 4.

What is the truth about Cole family beach vacations?

Repeated rounds of "By the Sea, the Beautiful Sea" always fill the car as the Cole family approaches Bethany Beach, Delaware. Excited about the week long vacation on the sandy shores, the four children speak in hyperbolic language about all the fun they will have.

However, within a few hours, the excitement turns to complaints about sunburns, collapsed sand castles, or airless rubber rafts.

Only parents John and Robyn are in touch with reality. They have not forgotten last summer's sand rashes or the aloe vera burn treatments. Still, armed with positive attitudes and high expectations, they continue to return year after year.

Parental control lost to computer technology

Guest editorial by Father John

Some may hail the computer age as the age of advancement, but parents, especially of teenagers, soon recognize that the introduction of computers into the home has diminished parental control.

How, you ask? A computer monomania develops. Once a computer enters the house, children are no longer content to sit passively and quietly in front of the television, or no longer find evenings of family board games entertaining.

If it doesn't involve e-mail or blood-and-guts computer game violence, it's considered simply boring.

The result is children who become so fixated on checking e-mail or playing computer games that all studies are abandoned and life is ennui.

Oh, for the days of my childhood when an evening playing Canasta, or watching "The Lone Ranger" was an exciting family activity!

Cole family accountant worries about expenses

Robyn Cole, wife of John Cole and mother of four teenage drivers, is alarmed at the high fuel bills that are depleting family resources.

Because she holds the dubious honor of family accountant, she must make difficult decisions about priorities in family spending. "Maintaining a balanced family budget is difficult with the runaway prices of gasoline," Cole said. "The situation is exacerbated by four teenage drivers."

In an effort to keep gas charges under control, Cole has taken to posting a daily account of expenditures on the refrigerator, underlining in red gas charges by the teenagers. "If they don't make an effort to control the charges, my husband and I will have to resort to drastic measures," Cole said. "My husband is ready to put one of the cars up on cinder blocks."

Evidence of the children's frustration was a sign in the front yard: COLE PARENTS UNFAIR TO CHILDREN! The sign at first went unnoticed by both parents, who always park their cars in the garage at the rear of the house. A neighbor alerted them when she asked what prompted it.

Both parents found the sign embarrassing. However, both agreed that it would take more than a sign in the front yard to change their minds. They do worry what that "something more" might be.

Cole family's Top Ten CDs
by Anne Cole

Influenced by our mother's diverse taste in music, we Cole family children rate the following CDs as our Top Ten:

- Everly Brothers' Hits
- Porgy and Bess
- Roger Miller Classics
- Brad Paisley Part Two
- Verdi's Rigoletto
- Beethoven's Fifth Symphony
- Bach's Magnificat
- Harp Music of Wales
- Charlotte Church's Voice of an Angel
- Paradise Road

Volume 1, Issue 2

Clark Family Gazette
Gettysburg, Pennslyvania

May 5, 2003

"Crazy curfew!" cry Clark kids

Talk of revolt in the air

"Eight o'clock is far too early for a curfew," according to Kerry Clark, age 16. "Most kids my age are able to be out until at least 11:00. Living here is like living in a convent!"

Mr. and Mrs. Clark, however, believe their restrictions are reasonable. "My roof, my rules!" bellows Mr. Clark. "When I was a lad, our curfew was 6:00 - and that was after we had to walk 4 miles uphill to school . . . in snow . . . both ways! Kids today are so soft and so lazy!"

According to Mrs. Clark, "If the children are out past a certain hour . . . well, that's when trouble starts to happen. We just want our babies to be safe." And that, according to Kerry, is partly the problem. "We're not 'babies' anymore," she responds. "I've become the laughing stock of the tenth grade! If my parents won't cave, I'm going to be forced to sneak out."

Adam Clark, 14, agrees. However, his ability to sneak out may be curbed by recent developments. (See related story, right.)

Trouble continues to brew at the Clark household. An impending revolt may be prevented, but both sides will need to act fast.

Adam Clark poses on the basketball court, before his skateboard injury.

Adam goes for broke!

Another unfortunate accident has befallen Adam, the eldest son of Mr. and Mrs. Clark. According to an anonymous source, he was attempting a new trick at Moe's Skatepark when he slipped and fell into the bowl, breaking his leg in three places.

This is the fourth serious injury sustained by Adam while skateboarding, and rumors abound that his parents are going to bar him from frequenting Moe's. Mr. and Mrs. Clark insist that a decision has not yet been made on the matter. "Let's get him home from the hospital first," they said tersely.

Kitten caboodle new focus of attention

Mitzi and Zoe, the feline pets at the Clark household, have both given birth to litters of kittens. Mitzi and Zoe, daughters of Panther (who met her untimely end in an encounter with a speeding Chevrolet), have shared many things in life, but never suspected that they would be beginning motherhood simultaneously!

Mitzi, proud mama to three calico babies, has staked out the area under the computer desk to be her nest, whereas Zoe, the black and white mother of two, has her brood wedged between the washer and dryer. "Looks like we won't be doing any laundry for a while!" cheered Bobby, age 10. Anyone interested in free kittens should call 888-555-1212 in about five weeks.

New kitten Cassie enjoys watching television.

writing and designing

SAMPLE FAMILY NEWSPAPER [PAGE 2]

Pancho Villa ranks high with Clark family

Clark Family Gazette, Page 2

Some say it's the ambience. Others say it's the food. Regardless, Pancho Villa is a huge hit with the entire Clark family. "Whenever we have a special occasion, we end up at Pancho Villa," Kerry explains. "It's the one restaurant that we all can agree on."

Upon entering the restaurant, it's easy to see why it has become such a favorite. The brightly colored Southwest décor cheerily greets patrons, and strains of the live Mariachi band playing "Guantanamera" filter through. Spicy aromas of tantalizing Mexican food tempt the taste buds.

Once seated, diners are immediately served complimentary chips and salsa to whet the appetite. Made freshly on the premises, the tortilla chips arrive warm. The most popular items on the menu for the Clark family include the garden burrito, a flour tortilla stuffed with a variety of fresh vegetables, and the chicken fajitas. The fajitas are sizzling strips of grilled chicken served with sautéed red bell peppers, onions, and mushrooms, topped with a choice of guacamole or sour cream. All items on the menu are available à la carte, or as complete dinners served with rice and beans.

What is the secret to making Pancho Villa so popular? "We are committed to using ingredients that are both fresh and healthy," owner Javier Gonzales claims. "We support our community's farmers by purchasing locally. Plus, our prices are very affordable."

That is certainly true. The à la carte dishes range from $1.95 to $3.50, and complete dinners start at $5.50. "We can afford to eat here sometimes," said Mrs. Clark. "And with all the free chips and large servings, we can even fill up Adam without going broke. Teenage boys are bottomless pits!"

Horoscope

Today

Aries: Beware of snitching on your siblings; it will come back to you.

Taurus: Persevere in your dreams and they will come true.

Gemini: Follow through with your obligations, both at home and at work.

Cancer: Romance blossoms! Aquarius prominent.

Leo: Trust your instincts.

Virgo: Be true to yourself and don't be influenced by the standards of others.

Libra: Travel to far-off exotic lands.

Scorpio: Focus on career and family.

Sagittarius: You may struggle with a difficult situation in regards to a friendship.

Capricorn: Avoid distraction when trying to complete your work.

Pisces: Be thrifty and save your allowance for a rainy day.

Annie's Advice Column

Dear Annie,
My little brother is such a pain! He's always rummaging through my belongings, and he recently read my diary. Now he's threatening to tell everyone at school all of my private, innermost secrets! What should I do?

Bothered by Bothersome Brother in Baltimore

Dear Bothered,
Ask your parents for a lock on your door. Also, it wouldn't hurt to remind your brother that you know all about the 1:00 a.m. peanut butter incident.

Annie

Dear Annie,
How can I get out of going to school?

Sick of It

Dear Sick of It,
Turn 18 and graduate.

Annie

Wanted: New sister

Anyone interested in a free sister, please contact "Annoyed Brother" at (888) 555-1212. All inquiries welcome. Will consider trade.

The good news is that everything is on the Internet.
The bad news is that everything is on the Internet.
— Dr. Robert Wachbroit,
Research Scholar at the School of Public Affairs,
Institute for Philosophy and Public Policy,
University of Maryland

When it conducted its first survey of the Internet in August of 1995, Netcraft, a major Internet consulting company, estimated there were fewer than 20,000 web sites in existence. By January 2002, over 36 million sites existed, and new web sites are now appearing at the rate of over four million a day. Another startling statistic is that 80 per cent of existing web sites are no more than one year old.

Creators of sites range from students of all ages to highly paid professional webmasters. Although amateurs create the majority of sites, they use sophisticated software that allows them to create professional appearing sites. Is it any wonder that individuals searching the web have difficulty discerning which sites contain reliable information when the packaging is so sophisticated?

Whether you like it or not, your students will most certainly be taking information from the Internet, so your major challenge is to help them develop and apply standards that determine the reliability of the information they find.

The excellent Wolfgram Memorial Library site includes some basic questions to help in evaluating a web page. The web address is:

http://www2.widener.edu/Wolfgram-Memorial-Library/webevaluation/webeval.htm

The authors, Jan Alexander and Marsha Ann Tate, use the five criteria listed below:

- **Authority.** Who is responsible for the site and its contents?
- **Accuracy.** Is the site accurate? Can sources be verified?
- **Objectivity.** Is the information based on fact or opinion? Are sources listed?
- **Currency.** Is the information up-to-date?
- **Coverage.** How complete and comprehensive is the information?

Distinguishing good sites from bad sites is not an easy task. The quality of the content and the reliability of a source are usually the most important factors for students to consider. However, as they gain experience evaluating, they will learn that overall design and ease of navigation are subtle but significant indicators of the quality of the web site as well.

The two following exercises will hone students' evaluation skills, giving them practice in selecting reliable web sites from which to take information for research assignments.

The first exercise, "Kinds of Web Sites," has them apply a set of standards based on the Wolfgram Memorial Library site. Alexander and Tate provide specific examples of five different kinds of web pages:

- personal
- advocacy
- business/marketing
- news
- informational

With the second exercise, "Evaluating Web Sites," students apply the five criteria discussed earlier. They also learn how to truncate the web address (URL) in order to determine the author or sponsor of the site when such information is not given.

Kinds of Web Sites

One of the problems of using the Internet for research is determining the credibility of the information you find. Judging the quality and accuracy of the information can be quite difficult. It helps to have a specific set of standards to apply consistently.

Fortunately, you don't have to come up with the standards on your own. Several web sites offer specific criteria you can apply. One of the best is the Wolfgram Memorial Library site at this address:

http://www2.widener.edu/Wolfgram-Memorial-Library/webevaluation/webeval.htm

The authors, Jan Alexander and Marsha Ann Tate, provide specific examples of five different kinds of web pages:

- personal
- advocacy
- business/marketing
- news
- informational

This exercise will help you learn to identify the different kinds of web sites, using the criteria above.

Step 1. Log on to the Internet and go to the Wolfgang Memorial Library web site. (See address above.) Quickly read about each of the five kinds of web pages.

Step 2. Open a new file and Save it as "Kinds of Web Sites."

Step 3. Now look up each of the web sites below. Determine what kind of web site it is, and label it in your document. (Toggle back and forth from your document to the Wolfgang Memorial Library page for help.)

(To toggle in Microsoft Word, choose **Window.** *A list of the Microsft Word documents that you have open will appear. Select the document you want to see. In later versions of Word, the titles of the various documents appear at the bottom of the screen. Simply click on whichever document you want to view.)*

www.gp.org	*www.peta.com*	*www.hud.gov*
www.johnnydeppfan.com/	*www.monster.com*	*www.rottentomatoes.com*
www.sprocketwire.com	*www.aclu.org*	*www.bordertelegraph.com*
www.zappos.com	*www.ratemykitten.com*	*www.presse.com.vu*
www.argusleader.com	*www.topozone.com*	*www.redcross.org*
www.ukonline.gov.uk	*www.orvis.com*	

Step 4. Save your work and Print two copies, one to keep and one to turn in.

Judging Web Sites

The following exercise is best used in conjunction with the previous exercise, "Kinds of Web Sites." Like the previous exercise, it relies on the criteria from the Wolfgang Memorial Library web site.

(See also teacher instructions for "Kinds of Web Sites," page 95.)

evaluating web sites

Judging Web Sites

Before you use information from a source either in a written or oral report, or even refer others to examine it, you need to be certain that the web site is a credible and noteworthy source. To do this, you need to determine who has created or sponsored the web site. The exercise that follows will help you determine a web site's value as a source.

Step 1. Log on to the Internet and use Yahoo, Google or Lycos to search. Type in your birthday, within quotation marks, like this: "March 2, 1985"

Step 2. Go to one of the sites identified in the search. Find its web address (URL) in the location line at the top of the window, with the prefix http://. Starting at the end of the URL, highlight the code to the first /. Then hit **Delete** to eliminate the last section of the address you have highlighted. Hit **Enter** to retrieve the new page.

Step 3. Examine the address of the page. Is it the same address, minus what you have deleted, or has it changed? Continue highlighting and deleting sections of the address until you reach the site's home page. As you delete, you may discover that sometimes an entirely new address may appear. A reliable web page should be linked to the site's sponsoring agent or individual if there is one. Knowing who sponsors a page can help you determine its reliability. The address itself can also give you information. For example, a site with a .gov suffix is a government site. Here are some more identifiers:

- .biz = business
- .com = commercial
- .edu = education
- .gov = government
- .info = information
- .mil = military
- .net = network
- .org = nonprofit organization

The address can also include a country code. For example, ".uk" indicates a site based in the United Kingdom, ".fr" indicates France, and ".ca" indicates Canada.

Step 4. Once you reach the home page or sponsoring web site, determine what type of web page it is. Is it a personal, advocacy, business/marketing, news, or informational page? Refer to the Wolfgang Memorial Library web site for a description of each type of site:

http://www2.widener.edu/Wolfgram-Memorial-Library/webevaluation/webeval.htm

Step 5. Next, find the evaluation questions at the Wolfgang Memorial Library web site for the kind of web site you have chosen. Read over the questions.

Step 6. Open a new document and Save it with the title "Birthday Web Sites." Put your name, class period, and date in the upper right-hand corner. Move down the page and type at the left the address of the web site you have chosen.

Step 7. Activate the numbering feature on your program and type the first evaluation question from the Wolfgang Memorial Library site.

(In Microsoft Word, click on the **Numbering icon** *on the* **Toolbar.** *It looks like a numbered list. Or go to* **Format,** *then* **Bullets and Numbering,** *and choose the numbering format you would like.)*

Use the question you just typed to evaluate the web site you have chosen. Type your answer right after your question.

Step 8. Type the next evaluation question and answer it. Repeat for each of the questions listed at the Wolfgang Memorial Library web site.

Step 9. Now choose two more web sites based on your birthday. Repeat steps 4-8, above. When you are finished, you should have a complete evaluation of three different web sites, using the criteria outlined for each type of site. Proofread your work. Save your work. Print two copies and hand in one.

"Internet Word Spy" is an activity that demonstrates the aliveness of the English language. New words are constantly being added to our vocabulary. Of course, some of the words have a short tenure, but many of them do indeed become a permanent part of the language. Some start out as specialized terms, but their meanings change as they become more commonly used. For example, a hundred years ago the term "input" was coined by physicists, but since then, because of computer technology, it has become a mainstream word used as both a noun and as a transitive verb. Purists may object, but it is now an entry in the Oxford English Dictionary.

For a fascinating look at newly-coined words and terms, take a look at the web site Word Spy! at *http://www.wordspy.com*. According to creator Paul McFredies, the site categorizes "recently coined words, existing words that have enjoyed a recent renaissance, and older words that are now being used in new ways." New words and definitions are added weekly, along with citations that show how the word is being used, background on the word's formation, a list of related words, and more.

Here is a list of words from past postings, but you may want to replace them with more recent examples on the site.

SAMPLE WORD SPY! LISTINGS

beeper-sitter: a person who assumes responsibility for recording another person's incoming beeper messages.

ladder gang: a roofing or painting company that calls on houses door-to-door and attempts to dupe homeowners into undergoing expensive and unnecessary repairs.

mycoremediation: the cleansing of a natural habitat by using fungi to break down harmful bacteria, toxic waste, and other impurities.

scam baiting: teasing a scam artist – particularly someone running the Nigerian advance fee fraud scheme – by feigning interest in the scam and forcing the scammer to perform silly or time-wasting tasks.

type T personality: a personality type that regularly seeks out thrilling or dangerous experiences.

Internet Word Spy

Where do new words come from? The web site Word Spy! will give you some clues. As described on its home page, this web site is "devoted to recently coined words and phrases, old words that are being used in new ways, and existing words that have enjoyed a recent renaissance." The words are not made up just for the web site. They are actual new words and phrases that have appeared in newspapers, magazines, books, press releases, and web sites.

Step 1. You have drawn a number assigning you to a team. Each team of three members has three words assigned to it. Each team member will be responsible for one of the words.

As your teammates do the same at different computers, log on to the Internet and go to the Word Spy! web site at *http://www.wordspy.com*.

Step 2. Search for the word you have been assigned. When you find it, Copy the definition.

Step 3. Open a new file and Save it as "Internet Word Spy." Then Paste the definition of your word. Then Copy and Paste the web address right below the definition. (Remember, any time you copy, you must give credit.)

Step 4. Go back to the web site and read the examples of the use of the word. Then go to your "Internet Word Spy" file and write your own original sentence using the word. Save your file to disk.

Step 5. Meet with your team members and choose a team captain. The captain should Open a new file, Save it as "Team Word Spy Results," and put your team members' names, class, and date in the upper right-hand corner of the page. He or she should type in the title "Word Spy Team Report" and center it.

Now the captain should Open all the documents the three team members have created and Copy and Paste them into the new document.

Step 6. Finally, as a team, work together to write a paragraph (or several) that incorporates all three of your assigned words. Make sure that your paragraph hints at the meaning of each of the words. This paragraph should be on page two of your document.

Step 7. When your paragraph is completed, Save it, and Print two copies.

Step 8. Trade paragraphs with another group. See if the group can guess the meanings of the new words simply by reading your paragraph.

Internet Thesaurus

"Internet Thesaurus" can help expand students' vocabularies, develop their writing skills, and increase their awareness of the usefulness of resource materials such as the thesaurus and the dictionary. At the same time, the activity provides them with supervised experience using the Internet as a source for information.

Although word lists are provided, you can easily substitute vocabulary words of your own choice. Once students have become acquainted with on-line dictionaries and thesauruses, encourage them to bookmark their favorites so they can easily access them when they are working on a paper. As you are certainly aware, students often skip using a thesaurus or a dictionary because one is not right at hand. Not so with an online source! Once bookmarked, it is only a mouse click away.

Internet Thesaurus

"Internet Thesaurus" is an exercise that will give you practice using an on-line dictionary and an on-line thesaurus. It will also challenge your imagination as you write a paragraph (or series of paragraphs) using all of the synonyms and antonyms you have found.

Step 1. Your teacher will either assign you a number or have you draw a number. Match your number to the appropriate word list, below.

List #1	List #2	List #3	List #4
acquittal	flagrant	keen	pace
apportionment	foil	knob	paradox
benevolence	gall	languish	rectify
bungler	gist	latitude	regenerate
cacophony	haughty	masquerade	scoff
coffer	heterogeneous	matrix	shrewd
docket	imagery	negotiate	verisimilitude
duplicity	indelible	notorious	vilify
embitter	jilt	officiate	literal
exceptional	juncture	overlook	thwart

Step 2. Open a new document Save it as "Internet Thesaurus." Put your name, class, and date in the upper right-hand corner of the page. Doublespace and center the title "Word List #_____," filling in the number of your word list. Doublespace again.

Step 3. Log on to the Internet and find an online dictionary. Here is one address you might try, but there are others as well:

http://www.yourdictionary.com

Define each word on your list. You may put each definition in your own words, or you may Copy and Paste a definition from the web site — as long as you put the definition you copy in quotation marks and list the web address where you found it. (See the example on page 105.)

Step 4. Next log on to an Internet thesaurus. Here is one address you might try, but there are others, as well:

http://www.thesaurus.com/

Find a synonym and an antonym for each word on your list. For a synonym, of course, you will want to choose a word with a meaning as close as possible to the original word. For an antonym, you will want to choose a word as close to opposite in meaning as possible. (See example on page 105.

expanding vocabulary

Step 5. Now create a short piece of writing that uses all of the words on your original list, as well as all of the antonyms and synonyms you have listed. You might write a paragraph or a short essay on a topic. You might relate an anecdote or write a short story. You might write a letter, tell a joke, write a movie review, or create any other piece of writing that you choose. Be sure to Bold each of the antonyms and synonyms that you use. Focus on writing sentences that effectively use each word. Do not include sentences like this one: "'Mastermind' is a word that means . . . ." See the example, below:

SAMPLE ENTRY

Mastermind: "A highly intelligent person, especially one who plans and directs a complex or difficult project."
[http://www.yourdictionary.com/ahd/m/m0142300.html]

Sentence: Scarface Joe was the mastermind of the bank robbery.

Synonym: genius

Antonym: idiot

Paragraph:

Some people thought that Oliver was an **idiot**. He was odd-looking and spoke very slowly and with an odd kind of rhythm to his speech. In reality, Oliver was truly a **genius**. At only eleven, he was the **mastermind** who came up with a plan that truly revolutionized the computer system used by his father's manufacturing company. Then, at twelve, he . . . . (etc.)

Step 6. When you have finished, Save. Print two copies of the report you have created. Turn in one copy and keep the other.

Step 7. Trade papers with someone who had the same group of words you did. Read that person's paper to see how someone else approached your assignment.

expanding vocabulary

Citing References

Students often have a misconception that information taken from the Internet is fair game. In other words, they believe they don't need to cite sources. Before beginning the next exercise, take time to review copyright law and plagiarism with your students. See the summary on page 109.

Note that the exercise gives students practice in informal documentation, using reference tags. For more formal documentation, students should follow a specific documentation format, such as the Modern Language Association (MLA) format described in the *MLA Handbook for Writers of Research Papers.* (See also "Documenting sources," page 128, of the Appendix.)

crediting sources

COPYRIGHT AND PLAGIARISM

What is plagiarism? Simply put, plagiarism is the theft of someone else's written words or ideas. Whenever you use information that is not your own, you must cite the source of the material. That includes information in any form: prose, poetry, dialogue from a play, charts, tables, etc. The information and the wording used to present it are both copyrighted.

Citations must be used whether you take the information from printed material like books and magazines or from the Internet. The reason for providing such citations is a simple one: copyright laws require you to do so. Copyright laws in the United States protect the creator of any work from unauthorized use of that work, even when the work has never been published. Furthermore, the creator does *not* have to display a copyright symbol to protect the work.

No one has the right to copy any part of another person or group's work without permission. An exception is made for short amounts used for educational purposes – as long as credit is given to the original.

What is common knowledge? A body of information that is considered *common knowledge* can be used without documentation. Common knowledge is information that is widely known or written about in a variety of sources. For example, widely publicized news accounts of honors bestowed on sports figures, movie stars, politicians, scientists, and other newsworthy individuals contain facts that can be considered common knowledge. So do accounts of past events like the Civil War, World War I, World War II, the dropping of the bomb on Hiroshima, President John F. Kennedy's Assassination, etc.

If you discover the same information in several accounts, you may make use of this information without crediting a source, as long as you can recount it without "leaning" on a source – in other words, without referring to the source frequently to help you phrase your ideas. If you do use specific phrasings unique to the sources you are using, you must cite the source.

If you are ever in doubt about the information being common knowledge, then cite the source. Use a reference tag to identify where you found it.

Citing References

Whenever you use information from another source in a report, a research paper, an article, or any other work, you must use citations to properly credit the source material you have used. If you don't, you are stealing another person or group's work or ideas and are guilty of plagiarism.

What are citations? They are simply references that document where the information you are using can be found. The citations used are of two kinds:

- Citations within the body of the paper
- A list of references at the end of the paper.

This exercise will give you practice in learning how to use citations.

Step 1. Choose a topic for a mini-research exercise. You may come up with a topic on your own or choose from the following broad topics:

gorillas	the Appalachian Trail
a famous fashion designer	yoga
the Eiffel Tower	the Wright brothers
elephants	canoes
the history of hip-hop music	Custer's last stand
a famous figure in sports	the saxophone
the Statue of Liberty	soccer

Step 2. Open a new document, and type your name, class and date in the upper right-hand corner. Then Save the document as "Research Notes."

Step 3. Log on to a search engine like Yahoo or Google and find 3-5 web sites with information on your topic. Copy their web addresses into your document. For example, if "Gorillas" were your topic, your page might look like this:

SAMPLE LISTING OF WEB SITE ADDRESSES

Gorilla web sites:

http://www.western-gorillas-eastern-gorillas.com

http://www.koko.org

http://www.unmuseum.org/fossey.htm

http://staff.washington.edu/timk/gorillas

http://www.enchantedlearning.com/subjects/apes/gorilla

Step 4. Now, look through the web sites to find an example of each of the following:

- A direct quotation from an authority or person directly involved with the subject you have chosen.

- A fact about your subject that is common knowledge. Remember: If something is common knowledge, it is a basic fact that can be found in many sources. If you use the fact, you must not use the language of any of your sources, unless you use quotation marks.

- Two or more phrases or sentences that contain interesting information about your subject. **Copy** the phrases or sentences and **Paste** them into your document, but remember to use quotation marks around them.

- A *paraphrased* paragraph of interesting information. (When you paraphrase, you put something into your own words, generally using about the same number of words as the original. You still need to credit your original source, so write your paraphrase under the web address where you found the original material.)

Copy and **Paste** each example into your document under the web address where you found it. (See example on page 112.)

Step 5. Write a paragraph or series of paragraphs that uses the information you have just listed. Be certain to use quotations marks whenever you are quoting a source exactly. (Remember that quotation marks always go outside periods and commas.)

Step 6. It is imperative that you provide citations in any formal or informal paper you write. Unless you are writing a formal research paper, it is usually quite acceptable to use within-text citations, often referred to as reference tags. (For more information about citations in formal research papers, see page 113.)

Reference tags are brief phrases that give enough information for the reader to locate the source — usually the author, title, and publication date. The following examples provide enough information for the reader to locate the original source.

- According to Rebecca Winters in an April 8, 2003, *Time* magazine article, a rain-forest plant native to South America, yerba mate, is becoming popular as a brewed alternative to tea and coffee. "Mate sippers credit the green tea-like drink, which has less caffeine than coffee, with fighting fatigue, aiding digestion and helping defog the brain," said Winters.

- Prescription drugs are sometimes tampered with as they pass through several middlemen on their way to the local pharmacy, reported *60 Minutes* correspondent Bob Simon in a December 20, 2002 broadcast.

- Bill Bryson, in his book *The Mother Tongue,* explains that the origins of the word "okay" are "so obscure that it has been a matter of heated dispute almost since it first appeared."

Now develop reference tags for the information you have used in your paragraph. Consider placing the reference tags in different places — not just at the beginning of the sentence.

Step 7. After you have a citation for every reference that requires one, Save and Print two copies of your paragraph (or paragraphs), one to keep and one to turn in to your teacher.

SAMPLE OF ITEMS CITED WITH WEB ADDRESSES

Gorilla web sites:

http://www.western-gorillas-eastern-gorillas.com/

Common knowledge: There are two kinds of gorillas: western and eastern.

http://www.koko.org/

Interesting information, paraphrased: The Gorilla Language Project involves teaching American Sign Language to two gorillas. Their names are Koko and Michael, but Michael recently passed away.

http://staff.washington.edu/timk/gorillas/

Quote from an authority: "The Cross River gorilla is a good example of why we must be very careful not to neglect possible diversity. In the nick of time we have realized these gorillas are distinct, just before it is finally too late to save them from oblivion," said Dr. John F. Oates, primatologist with Hunter College - CUNY."

Interesting information: The Uganda Wildlife Authority (UWA) and its counterparts in Rwanda and the Democratic Republic of Congo, have petitioned Interpol to investigate and arrest suspects engaged in poaching of the highly endangered mountain gorillas.

http://www.enchantedlearning.com/subjects/apes/gorilla/

Interesting information: "Gorillas each have a unique nose print (like we have unique fingerprints)."

Interesting information: "Newborn gorillas weigh only about 3-4 pounds (1.4 to 1.8 kg) at birth (about half the weight of a newborn human)."

FORMAL DOCUMENTATION

If you are writing a formal research paper, the practice is to use a formal style of documentation, according to a particular documentation source. The Modern Language Association of America (MLA) and the American Psychological Association (APA) publish two of the most commonly used style sheets. These systems have very specific rules of documentation. (See *ww.mla.org* and *www.apa.org*.) See also "Useful Online References," page 140.

So Say the Critics

Looking for a warm-up research paper writing assignment that also develops students' Internet search skills? "So Say the Critics" fits the bill. It has students write a short paper reporting on what critics have to say about a film.

Of course, you will want to approve each student's choice of a film. You may even want to develop a list for students to select from, perhaps selecting only movies developed from classics. (There are enough movie versions of Shakespearean plays that you might even restrict their search to them.)

If you do allow students to select recent films, you should direct them to check listings of films playing at major theaters. As you know, the web sites created by theater conglomerates also link reviews of films. This makes the searching perhaps too easy, but the reviews are usually reputable ones.

As you will see when you review the step-by-step instructions, this activity emphasizes note taking, so make certain that students don't skip this step. Understanding the information they find in their searches is key to their writing good summaries and paraphrases. Without taking notes, students don't usually develop such a command of the information and end up unintentionally plagiarizing.

So Say the Critics

Do you read movie reviews? Perhaps more of us ought to. Then we might not be so disappointed after spending good money to see a film or rent a video, and then hating it!

In this writing assignment, you will gain some practice researching, writing and citing sources, all through searching the Internet for reviews of recent movies.

Before you begin, you will need to select a movie. Don't select anything that has just been released, and try not to go back more than five years, unless you select a blockbuster like *E.T.* or *Star Wars*. Once your teacher approves your film choice, you are ready to begin.

Step 1. Open a new document and Save it as "So Say the Critics."

Step 2. Put your name, class, and date in the upper right-hand corner of your document and title it "What the Critics Say about *Name of Film*."

Step 3. Open a second document and Save it as "Film Notes." Minimize both documents.

Step 4. Search the Internet for reviews of the movie you have selected. You are on your own in thinking of key words to use for searching. However, simply entering "review of *Name of Film*" should lead to many results in most search engines like Yahoo! and Google. When you find a source, Bookmark it. Then find at least two more sites with reviews of your movie, and Bookmark those, too.

(In Microsoft Internet Explorer, go to Favorites in the Menu and choose Add a Favorite. Then choose a name for your selection.)

Step 5. Go to your Favorites folder and open the first review. Copy and Paste the web address (URL) into your "Film Notes" document. Also Copy and Paste other source information such as the author and title of the review.

Step 6. Read the review and take notes. How does the reviewer feel about the film? Summarize his or her opinion. Also Copy and Paste any information you would like to quote from the review. Remember to include quotation marks around anything you copy, to remind you that it is not in your own words.

Step 7. Repeat Step 6 with each of the remaining reviews.

Step 8. Now, using your notes, write a short paper that reports on the critics' view of the film you have chosen. You might imagine that you are giving an overview of the critics' opinions for someone interested in the film. Be sure to mention the critics by name and provide quotations that represent their differing styles of criticism.

Step 9. As you write your paper, be very careful not to plagiarize. Use reference tags when you quote, paraphrase, or summarize information from the sources. As a reminder, reference tags provide enough information so that the reader of your paper can find the reviews. Here are two examples:

- According to J. Hoberman in the December 19-25, 2001, issue of *The Village Voice*, the movie *Lord of the Rings*: *The Fellowship of the Ring* is "certainly successful on its own terms."

- "The movie depends on action scenes much more than Tolkien did," said Roger Ebert in his December 19, 2001, review of *The Lord of the Rings*: *The Fellowship of the Ring* in the *Chicago Sun Times*.

Step 10. Because you have taken your information from the Internet, create a Works Cited page to follow your paper. Your teacher will refer you to an online style manual to follow.

(Many teachers prefer the MLA Style Manual. You can find information about it at www. mla.org. An example of a "Works Cited" page can be found on page 111.)

Step 11. After you have finished your draft, proofread and edit. Then run Spelling check.

(In Microsoft Word, go to **Tools** *on the* **Menu** *bar and select* **Spelling and Grammar . . .** *)*

Step 12. Save your work. Print two copies — one to keep and one to turn in.

Birth Booklet

"Birth Booklet" provides students an opportunity to share their roots as well as their interests with their classmates. It also gives them additional experience researching a topic using Internet sources.

Although not a traditional research assignment, "Birth Booklet" is an excellent warm-up activity to researching a topic for an MLA or APA style research paper. While completing the activity, students gain experience copying and pasting information from a variety of sources — and, as the directions make clear, identifying and listing the web sites from which they obtain their information. They then face the challenge of reformatting the material to fit the design of their booklet. The sample booklets illustrate both landscape and portrait layouts.

You may also want to encourage those students whose computer skills are more advanced to consider a folded layout where they divide one standard landscape page that is 11" by 8 ½ " into two pages that are 5 ½" by 8 ½ " when folded. If they create a folded brochure, they should set half inch margins at the top, bottom, and outside edges.

EXAMPLE OF A BOOKLET WITH ONE FOLDS

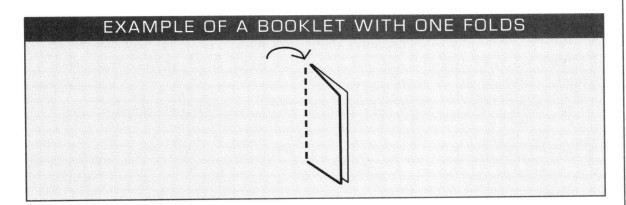

A booklet with two folds, like a brochure, is also a possibility. See the instructions for creating a brochure in the "Myth Brochure" activity, pages 81 and 82.

"Birth Booklet" is one activity you may also want to do yourself so that you can share some of the important events from your own roots.

Birth Booklet

What was happening in the world during a very important year — the year you were born? With "Birth Booklet," you will use the Internet to gather information about your birth year. Then you will create a booklet about your birth year, based on your findings.

Step 1. Open a new document and Save it as "Birth Booklet Notes." Then Minimize the document and log on to the Internet.

Step 2. Search the Internet for events happening the year of your birthday. You may want to experiment with what key words to use in your search. Simply using the year of your birth will give you millions of matches. You might want to use the actual day of your birth, or you might want to look for the year of your birth in conjunction with specific subject areas, for example, "1985 and sports," or "1985 and books." Whenever you find information or photographs that you would like to include in your booklet, Copy the web address (URL) of the site into your "Birth Booklet Notes" document. Then Copy and Paste the information you want to use under the web address.

Step 3. Continue searching web sites until you have collected a wide variety of interesting material. Be sure to Copy the web address of each site before you Copy and Paste the information you want to use. Also remember to use quotation marks around any material that you quote exactly. (If you put material into your own words, you don't need the quotation marks. You still need the web address, though.)

Step 4. Now you are going to create a 4-6 page booklet about your birth year. It should provide a detailed characterization of your birth year, represented by your selection of pictures and information. It should also reflect your personality and interests. For example, if you are an avid reader, you might want to include information about books popular at that time. If you love music, you might want to include information about music of the era. If you love ice hockey, you might want to include more information about that sport.

Here are some ideas for items you might include in your booklet:

- headlines in the news
- advertisements of the day
- economic details
- historical events
- scientific breakthroughs
- inventions
- elected officials
- scandals
- family events

- popular culture (television shows, movies, books, etc.)
- famous people born that year
- odd facts or items of interest

You might also consider adding scanned family photographs from the time of your birth.

Step 5. The format of the booklet is up to you. However, it should have a cover, an index, and several pages of text and pictures. The final page of the book should be a list of the web addresses for each piece of information included in the booklet.

Booklets should be as varied as individuals. Two sample brochures are included on pages 120-132.

Step 6. When you are pleased with your brochure, Save again. Then Print copies — one to hand in and one for yourself. You may also want to print extra copies for family members.

SAMPLE BIRTH BOOKLET #1 (PAGE 1)

Tracy Atkins
Birth Booklet
28 March 2003

Significant
Events of
My Birth Year
1988

researching and writing

SAMPLE BIRTH BOOKLET #1 (PAGE 2)

Table of Contents

Most Significant Family Events of 1988: Birth, Homecoming, Accident   3

Two Other Significant Family Events of 1988   4

Other Facts from 1988   5

Significant World Events of 1988   6

Works Cited   7

Most Significant Family Events of 1988:
Birth, Homecoming, Accident

At precisely 11:03 p.m. EST on Tuesday, June 16, 1988, Roberta Hull-Atkins gave birth to her fourth child, a six pound, eleven ounce brunette girl. An admirer of singer Tracy Chapman, Roberta named her second daughter Tracy. Roberta was almost as delighted by Chapman winning Grammies in 1988 as Best New Artist and Best Pop Vocal by a Female as she was by the birth of her second daughter. Tracy's father James approved the name, as Chapman's song "Fast Car" was one of his favorites.

Three days later, baby Tracy arrived home, greeted by her siblings – her brothers Russell and James and her sister Melinda. They greeted her at the door and kept peeking in on her all day as they were so excited to have a new sister. However, her ride from the hospital was most annoying to her elder brother Russell, as he wanted to be the first Atkins child to ride home in the new car, a 1988 Toyota Camry.

Tracy is greeted by siblings waiting at the front door.

On the morning after Tracy's first night at home, June 20, 1988, Dad Atkins wrecked the new car. He awoke exhausted, having been up most of the night holding Tracy. Although he drove as carefully as he could to make it to work, he was so fatigued from walking the floor with Tracy during the night that he never saw the other car pull onto the highway. Stomping on the brakes, he careened off the road into an old stump. The car was severely damaged. Fortunately, he was not hurt. However, that was no consolation to him.

SAMPLE BIRTH BOOKLET #1 (PAGE 4)

Two Other Significant Family Events of 1988

A week after Tracy's arrival home, the family celebrated her brother Russell's sixth birthday with a party in the back yard. Mom baked him a special cake in the shape of the Tin Man, his favorite character from *The Wizard of Oz*, a movie the whole family loved. Tracy also grew to love the film, but her favorite character was Dorothy.

Two weeks later, there was more excitement in the Atkins household when the children welcomed new-born kittens into the family. The pet cat Mouse delivered four healthy kittens: three girls and a boy. Mouse was a doting mother. She insisted on having her kittens in the parents' bedroom in a cardboard box so they

had the protection of Mother Roberta and Father James. The kittens were the center of attention, so much so that Dad eventually moved to the pull-out bed in the family room to get a good night's sleep. He simply couldn't stand the purring and meowing that was constant through the night.

Fortunately, the car accident was the only setback for the Atkins family in 1988. There were many interesting world events that unfolded during the first year of Tracy's life as a member of the family. These events are documented on the following pages of this booklet.

researching and writing

SAMPLE BIRTH BOOKLET PAGE 5

Other Facts from 1988

Top Grossing Movies of 1988

#1 Rain Man

#2 Who Framed Roger Rabbit?

#3 Coming to America

#4 Big

#5 Twins

Panamanian Dictator Manuel Noriega was arrested, tried, and convicted for drug trafficking.

Top Ten Singles of 1988

- "Faith," by George Michael
- "Need You Tonight," by INXS
- "Got My Mind Set On You," by George Harrison
- "Never Gonna Give You Up," by Rick Astley
- "Sweet Child O' Mine," by Guns N Roses
- "So Emotional," by Whitney Houston
- "Heaven Is a Place On Earth," by Belinda Carlisle
- "Could've Been," by Tiffany
- "Hands to Heaven," by Breathe
- "Roll With It," by Steve Winwood

SAMPLE BIRTH BOOKLET #1 (PAGE 6)

Significant World Events of 1988

- CDs outsell vinyl for the first time ever.
- Soviets leave Afghanistan.
- Summer Olympics in Seoul, South-Korea; Ben Johnson is charged with steroids use after setting a world record in the 100 meter dash.
- Pan Am Flight 103 explodes over Lockerbie, Scotland; Libyan terrorists are suspected of planting the bomb.
- Earthquake in the USSR.
- Bobby McFerrin tells everyone "Don't worry, be happy."
- Prozac is introduced as an anti-depressant.
- US advertising is permitted on Soviet TV.
- The first plutonium pacemaker is made.
- World's longest undersea tunnel is completed. Work begins on the Chunnel.

researching and writing

SAMPLE BIRTH BOOKLET #1 (PAGE 7)

Works Cited

"Big News Headlines in 1988."
http://spiffyentertainment.8m.com.1988mem.html>22March 2003

"Famous Mugshots: Celebrities and the Famous Behind Bars."
http://www.mugshots.org/misc.manuel-noriega.html>22March 2003

"Grammy Awards 1988: Parents Just Don't Understand."
http://80music.about.com/library/grammy/bl_1988.htm 22March 2003

"Oz Net Music Chart"
http://www.onmc.iinet.net.au/USA/usa1988.htm

"Superbowl Surprise 1988."
http://www.forerunner.com?X0767_Super_Bowl_Surprise_.html>22March 2003

"Timeline of the 80s 1988."
http://www.inthe80s.com/time1988.shtml?22March 2003

1985: A GOOD YEAR

Jacob Smith
Birth Booklet
May 8, 2003

SAMPLE BIRTH BOOKLET #2 (PAGE 2)

TABLE OF CONTENTS

Most Significant Family Events of 1985…………….......3

Some Significant World Events of 1985……………....4

Miscellaneous Facts About My Family……………......5

Entertainment Facts For 1985………………………....5

Works Cited…..…………………………………….....6

SAMPLE BIRTH BOOKLET #2 (PAGE 3)

Most Significant Family Events of 1985

#1: HAPPY BIRTHDAY TO ME!
My birthday was the most significant family event of 1985. Nothing else that cool happened that year! I was born at St. Mary's Hospital in Sioux Falls, South Dakota, at 2:15 p.m. on July 10th, 1985. When I was born, I weighed seven pounds and two ounces. I am really glad that my birthday is in the summer. I always have a pool party because I love to swim.

#2: The second most significant family event that happened the year I was born was the family reunion. It was held at a lakeside resort. I was of course a little baby and don't remember anything about it, but I've seen the pictures and it is amazing how many people were there. Everyone enjoyed swimming, fishing, boating, and playing Yahtzee. There is one photo from the reunion that is my all-time favorite. It is a picture of my Aunt Dee holding me and smiling. She is really cool. She is like sixty-something now and is still so adventurous. She goes on trips everywhere from Iceland to Australia. She is always planning her next trip. I love to hear the stories she has about all the places she visits.

Uncle Jim and
Cousin Kelly

Fishing off the dock at the family reunion

#3: The third most significant family event of my birth year was when my mom and dad bought a parrot. They named it Fred and it was our family pet for about ten years until it died of old age. Fred was quite the talker. He was a funny bird! We all loved him very much. Good old Fred.

Fred

SAMPLE BIRTH BOOKLET #2 [PAGE 4]

Some Significant World Events of 1985

Mikhail Gorbachev replaces Soviet leader Chernenko, following his death at the age of 73. Gorbachev begins a program of reform. *(http://www.factmonster.com/year/1985.html)*

Terrorists of the Palestine Liberation Organization hijack the Italian cruise ship, the Achille Lauro. Eighty passengers plus the crew of the ship are held hostage. An American, Leon Klinghoffer, is killed. *(http://www.factmonster.com/year/1985.html)*

The LIVE AID concerts are held in London, England; Philadelphia, Pennsylvania; Moscow, Russia; and Sydney, Australia, to benefit victims of famine in Africa. *(http://www.inthe80s.com/time1985.shtml)*

Olaf Palme, Swedish premier, is assassinated. *(http://www.inthe80s.com/time1985.shtml)*

A new rating, PG-13, is established by the Motion Picture Association of America. *(http://www.decades.com/ByDecade/1980-1989/41.htm)*

The Giotto space probe gave the world a close-up of Halley's Comet. *(http://www.decades.com/ByDecade/1980-1989/41.htm)*

Ronald Reagan begins his second term as President of the U.S. *(http://www.factmonster.com/year/1985.html)*

SAMPLE BIRTH BOOKLET #2 (PAGE 5)

Miscellaneous Facts About My Family

- My grandma Celeste once met Jimmy Carter.
- I had to have my tonsils and my wisdom teeth taken out in the same year!
- My mom used to be on a synchronized swimming team at her college.
- My dad taught our dog how to roll over in only two tries!
- My family's favorite meal is pot roast.
- I love basketball!!!!

Entertainment Facts for 1985

THE TOP MOVIES OF 1985:

Back to the Future

Rambo: First Blood Part II

Rocky IV

The Color Purple

Out of Africa

Cocoon

The Jewel of the Nile

Witness

The Goonies

Police Academy 2: Their First Assignment

(http://80music.about.com/library/1980s/bl_topmovies-1985.htm)

1985 GRAMMY AWARDS

Record of the Year was "We Are the World," by USA for Africa.

Album of the year was *No Jacket Required*, by Phil Collins.

Song of the Year was "We Are the World," by Michael Jackson and Lionel Richie.

Best New Artist was Sade.

(http://www.factmonster.com/year/1985.html)

researching and writing

SAMPLE BIRTH BOOKLET #2 (PAGE 6)

Works Cited

http://www.decades.com/ByDecade/1980-1989/41.htm

http://www.factmonster.com/year/1985.html

http://www.inthe80s.com/time1985.shtml

http://80music.about.com/library/1980s/bl_topmovies-1985.htm

APPENDIX

Internet Terms

One of the most comprehensive and frequently updated lists of Internet terms appears on Matisse Enzer's web site:

http://www.matisse.net/files/glossary.html

Enzer allows teachers to use this glossary for non-commercial educational purposes. He asks only that any reproduction be credited to Matisse Enzer and that teachers duplicating it not alter the content. He also allows links to the web site without seeking permission to link.

Online Internet dictionaries are also excellent for defining unknown Internet terms. Here is a list of helpful sites:

- *http://www.webopedia.com/*

- *http://www.whatis.com/*

- *http://www.netlingo.com/inframes.cfm*

- *http://foldoc.doc.ic.ac.uk/foldoc/index.html*

- *http://www.internettermsdictionary.com/*

- *http://www.thirdage.com/features/tech/glossary/*

- *http://www.msg.net/kadow/answers/*

- *http://www.whaddup.com/dictionary/index.htm*

Online Writing Labs

Online writing labs, often referred to by the acronym OWL, provide writing resources and one-on-one advice from qualified writers. The most well known is the Purdue Online Writing lab:

http://owl.english.purdue.edu/

In addition to providing numerous resources for writing, the Purdue OWL hyperlinks 50 online writing labs. Here are just a few of them.

http://www.rscc.cc.tn.us/OWL/owl.html
Roane State Community College in Harriman, Tennessee, includes an article providing tips on developing a cyberspace writing center, one where students e-mail papers back and forth for advice on revision.

http://writing.colostate.edu/
The Writing Center at Colorado State University provides a wide range of guides for writers, each designed to help a writer find information quickly on a given topic. It also includes interactive tutorials and demonstrations, links to other useful sites, guides for teachers, and much more.

http://depts.gallaudet.edu/Englishworks/
The Gallaudet University OWL called "English Works!" provides an extensive list of exercises and resources to guide students through the writing of a paper, the reading of a work, or the study of a particular piece of literature. Because of the detailed step-by-step approach, many of the exercises are especially useful for remedial situations.

http://www.english.uga.edu/~writingcenter/home.html
The University of Georgia Writing Center web site includes a "Writer Resources" index that provides excellent exercises and guides for every aspect of the writing process.

http://www.english.uiuc.edu/cws/wworkshop/writer.html
The University of Illinois Writers' Workshop web site has a comprehensive Tips and Techniques section plus an annotated list of the best sites for writers.

Interactive Internet sites require the visitor to participate in some activity. The visitor may have to play an online game, click on certain buttons to complete a story, or make selections from a list of pictures or texts to open up for viewing or reading. The numerous interactive Internet language and literature activities available online provide teachers with an opportunity to re-engage students who are accustomed to more bells and whistles than a text-based curriculum can provide.

One of the most popular interactive lessons is the WebQuest, a teaching model developed by Bernie Dodge and Tom March at San Diego State University in 1995. A WebQuest is an inquiry-oriented lesson that has students drawing most or all the information used in the activity from the Internet. The focus is on using information, rather than looking for it.

Interactive lessons are here to stay. Unfortunately, individual web sites are relatively unstable, so it is impossible to know for certain which interactive sites will be available from month to month. Used to enhance the reading and study of literature, interactive sites can add a dimension of both entertainment and reinforcement to the traditional classroom study of literature and language. They can also provide additional writing opportunities that often prove more engaging for students than many traditional exercises.

Here are a few sites, available as this book went to press, that provide excellent information about interactive Internet lessons:

http://www.kn.pacbell.com/wired/bluewebn/categories.html
Conceived of by Jodi Reed and sponsored by Bell, Blue Web'n is a hyperlinked database of over 1,000 blue ribbon Internet learning sites categorized by subject area, audience, and type.

http://webquest.sdsu.edu/
Developed by San Diego State University, this web site lists 64 WebQuests for teachers wanting to use the WebQuest model. As defined on the web site, a WebQuest is "an inquiry-oriented activity in which most or all of the information used by learners is drawn from the Web. WebQuests are designed to use learners' time well, to focus on using information rather than looking for it, and to support learners' thinking at the levels of analysis, synthesis and evaluation. The model was developed in early 1995 at San Diego State University by Bernie Dodge with Tom March."

http://www.nationalgeographic.com/salem
An excellent example of an interactive Internet lesson suitable for the English/language arts classroom, this National Geographic web site provides students reading *The Crucible* or studying Cotton Mather's accounts of the Salem witch trials a first hand simulated experience as an accused witch.

http://www.memphis-schools.k12.tn.us/admin/tlapages/lesson-template.htm
This site provides a model, created by a Memphis teacher, for creating a WebQuest.

http://schools.sd68.bc.ca/webquests/
This site provides general information about WebQuests.

http://school.discovery.com/schrockguide/
This site, created by Kathy Schrock, includes a categorized list of hundreds of WebQuests, as well as samples of WebQuests.

http://www.spa3.k12.sc.us/WebQuests.html
This site provides general information about using WebQuests, as well as WebQuests created by teachers in the Spartanburg School District 3 in South Carolina.

Some popular search engines are listed below. However, new ones appear regularly and others disappear. An Internet search can give you the most up-to-date list.

beaucoup.com

goto.com

hotbottom. com

altavista.com

google. com

inferencefind.com

dogpile.com

yahoo.com

boingo.com

metacrawler.com

lycos.com

askjeeves.com

Popular Search Engines

Boolean search methods

Using Boolean search methods can lead to more precise and effective Internet searches. An excellent source of information on Boolean search methods is at this address:

http://webquest.sdsu.edu/searching/sevensteps.html

Called "Seven Steps for Better Searching," the site guides students through seven phases of searching, using catchy mnemonic labels to help the student remember how to search properly. Each phase involves a refining of the research process and requires students to record the results of the searching before going on to the next phase.

Another very useful web site is Albany University Library's "Boolean Searching on the Internet":

http://library.albany.edu/internet/boolean.html

While providing a detailed discussion of the concept of Boolean searching, it also explains which search engine to use for the various Boolean features.

Useful Online References

Online resources can be very helpful in the English classroom. The following web sites were in operation as this book was published:

Documenting sources

http://www.santarosa.edu/library/guides/mla.shtml

The web site is sponsored by Santa Rosa Junior College in California. It provides excellent examples of MLA format.

Research

http://www.ipl.org/ref/

A virtual warehouse of resources is The Internet Public Library (IPL). The collection is an annotated list of authoritative resources that are frequently used and regularly updated. The IPL also has an original resource called "A+ Research & Writing for High School and College Students": *http://www.ipl.org/teen/aplus/*. It provides excellent step-by-step assistance in finding information and writing a research paper.

Copyright issues

http://www.loc.gov/copyright/
http://www.eff.org/pub/Intellectual_property/
These sites include a great deal of information about copyright issues.

Online help

http://www.askanexpert.com/
Ask an Expert is a directory of links to 300 individuals who have volunteered to answer questions from young people. The 300 web sites and e-mail addresses are categorized under the headings Science and Technology, Career and Industry, Health, Internet and Computers, Recreation, Entertainment, International and Cultural, Resources, Money and Business, Fine Arts, Law, Religion, and Education and Personal Development.

John O. Cole is an associate professor of English at West Liberty State College in West Liberty, West Virginia, where he has taught composition and English education courses for the past 35 years. He also has experience teaching at the high school level.

Currently, he is the director of composition at WLSC and serves as president of the West Virginia English Language Arts Council, a state affiliate of the National Council of Teachers of English.

From 1980 to 2000, he served as mayor of Bethany, West Virginia, the home of Bethany College, where his wife of 35 years teaches composition and linguistics. The Coles have four children.

About the Author

Ordering Information

To Order More Copies of Plugged In to English

Please send me _____ copies of *Plugged In to English*. I am enclosing $28.95, plus shipping and handling ($4.50 for one book, $1.00 for each additional book). Colorado residents add 83¢ sales tax per book. Total amount $_____. Each copy also comes with a CD-ROM.

Name _____

(School) _____
(Include only if using school address.)

Address _____

City _____ State _____ Zip Code _____

Method of Payment:

❑ Payment enclosed   ❑ Visa/MC/Discover   ❑ Purchase Order *(Please attach.)*

Credit Card# _____Expiration Date _____

Signature _____

Send to:

Cottonwood Press, Inc.
107 Cameron Drive
Fort Collins, CO 80525
1-800-864-4297
www.cottonwoodpress.com

Call for a free catalog of practical materials for
English and language arts teachers, grades 5-12.